SWU-NAP- 017

# UNIFORMS OF RUSSIAN ARMY DURING THE NAPOLEONIC WAR VOL.12

### UNDER THE REIGN OF ALEXANDER I
### EMPEROR OF RUSSIA BETWEEN 1801 AND 1825
ARTILLERY: FOOT, HORSE AND GARRISON ARTILLERY

From the Viskovatov's greatest work:
"Historical description of the clothing and
arms of the Russian Army"

English translation by Mark Conrad

## SOLDIERSHOP PUBLISHING

## AUTHOR

Aleksandr Vasilevich Viskovatov born 22 April (4 May New Style) 1804, died 27 February (11 March) 1858 in St. Petersburg, Russian military historian. He graduated from the 1st Cadet Corps and served in the artillery, the hydrographic depot of the Naval Ministry, and then in the Department of Military Educational Institutions. He mainly studied historical artifacts and the histories of military units. Viskovatov's greatest work was the Historical Description of the Clothing and Arms of the Russian Army.

## PUBLISHING'S NOTE

## NOTE ABOUT BOOK PRINTING BEFORE 1925

## LICENSES COMMONS

## ACKNOWLEDGEMENTS

A Special Thanks to NYPL and other institutions for their kindly permission to use some images of his archives, collections or books used in our book.

Title: **UNIFORMS OF RUSSIAN ARMY DURING THE NAPOLEONIC WAR VOL. 12**
Artillery_ Foot, Horse and Garrison Artillery
By A.V.Viskovatov. Serie edit by Luca S. Cristini. First edition by Soldiershop. August 2017
Cover & Art Design: Luca S. Cristini. Plates re-colorations by Anna Cristini.
ISBN code: 978-88-93272636
Published by Soldiershop publishing, via Padre Davide, 7 - 24050 Zanica (BG) ITALY. www.soldiershop.com

# UNIFORMS
# OF THE RUSSIAN ARMY
# DURING THE NAPOLEONIC
# WAR  VOL. 12

## UNDER THE REIGN OF ALEXANDER I EMPEROR OF
## RUSSIA BETWEEN 1801 AND 1825

\*

## ARTILLERY: FOOT, HORSE AND GARRISON ARTILLERY

*Alexander I of Russia in a portrait by G. Dawe (1826, Peterhof)*

# HISTORICAL DESCRIPTION OF THE CLOTHING AND ARMS OF THE RUSSIAN ARMY - A.V. VISKOVATOV

### (First English translation by Mark Conrad)

Soldiershop is glad to presents the complete collection of the great job made by A.V. Viskovatov dedicated to the uniforms and weapons belonging to the Russian army during the Napoleonic period, until 1825. The time we considered corresponds to the reigns of two Tzars: Paul I, who reigned since 1769 until his murder on the 23rd of March 1801, and his son Aleksandr Pavlovič Romanov, that with the title of Alexander I, sat on the throne until the 1st December 1825.

Our reprint in based on the original 19th century volumes, to be precise the volumes from 7 to 9 are dedicated to the reign of Paul I; this first part is distributed on 7 volumes, having a numbering from 1 to 7. From number 10 to 18 of the original volumes, the second part is dedicated to the Russian troops under Alexander I. These still being worked on and they will be soon ready, distributed on twenty volumes approximately. Our new edition, the first ever published in English, both on paper and digital format, boasts a large number of color plates, many of them unpublished and coloured by our team of expert artists and scholars of uniformology. Each volume is based on 50/70 plates, always accompanied by the original translated text which describes the uniforms, the organization and the armament of the Russian army of the period.

A unique work in its genre, a must have in any respecting collection!

Aleksandr Vasilevich Viskovatov born 22 April (4 May New Style) 1804, died 27 February (11 March) 1858 in St. Petersburg, Russian military historian. He graduated from the 1st Cadet Corps and served in the artillery, the hydrographic depot of the Naval Ministry, and then in the Department of Military Educational Institutions.

He mainly studied historical artifacts and the histories of military units. Viskovatov's greatest work was the Historical Description of the Clothing and Arms of the Russian Army (Vols. 1-30, St. Petersburg, 1841-62; 2nd ed. Vols. 1-34, St. Petersburg - Novosibirsk - Leningrad, 1899-1948). This work is based on a great quantity of archival documents and contains four thousand colored illustrations.

Viskovatov was the author of Chronicles of the Russian Army (Books 1-20, St. Petersburg, 1834-42) and Chronicles of the Russian Imperial Army (Parts 1-7, St. Petersburg, 1852). He collected valuable material on the history of the Russian navy which went into A Short Overview of Russian Naval Campaigns and General Voyages to the End of the XVII Century (St. Petersburg, 1864; 2nd edition Moscow, 1946). Together with A.I. Mikhailovskii-Danilevskii he helped prepare and create the Military Gallery in the Winter Palace.

He wrote the historical military inscriptions for the walls of the Hall of St. George in the Great Palace of the Kremlin. (From the article in the Soviet Military Encyclopedia.)

# CONTENTS

*

# RUSSIAN ARMY- ARTILLERY: FOOT, HORSE AND GARRISON ARTILLERY

CHANGES IN THE CLOTHING AND ARMAMENTS OF ARMY AND GARRISON ARTILLERY, ARMY SAPPERS AND PIONEERS, FIELD AND GARRISON ENGINEERS, MILITARY LABOR BATTALIONS AND COMPANIES, HIS IMPERIAL MAJESTY'S SUITE FOR QUARTERMASTER AFFAIRS, AND TOPOGRAPHERS, FROM 1801 THROUGH 1825:

VIII. Army Foot Artillery
IX.   Army Horse Artillery
X.  Garrison Artillery
Notes.

## ARMY ARTILLERY

**27 August 1801**– From the seven Foot and one Horse regiment which made up the Field Artillery [*Polevaya Artilleriya*] were formed *Artillery Battalions*: the *1st, 2nd, 3rd, 4th, 5th, 6th, 7th, 8th, 9th, 10th, 11th, 12th,* and *13th,* and a *Horse-Artillery Battalion* (173).

**19 March 1803**– These battalions, increased by an additional five new ones, were each brought to an establishment of two Battery [*Batareinaya,* meaning Heavy or Positional] companies and two Light [*Legkaya*] companies, and from all these, combined by twos, were formed *Artillery Regiments: 1st, 2nd, 3rd, 4th, 5th, 6th, 7th, 8th,* and *9th.* The Horse Artillery was increased with one more battalion, the *2nd Horse-Artillery Battalion [2-i Konno-Artilleriiskii batalion],* and the previous one was named the *1st* (174).

**4 June 1804**– From the Pontoon Depots there was formed an *Artillery Pontoon Regiment [Artilleriiskii Pontonnyi polk],* made up of two four-company battalions (175).

**31 August 1805**– Two more Artillery regiments were formed: the *10th* and *11th,* on the same basis as the previous ones (176).

**23 August 1806**– The Artillery regiments were disbanded, including the Pontoon Regiment and Horse battalions, and in their place were established *brigades [brigady]* (corresponding to the number and designations of Artillery divisions and Inspectorates), with the following numbers of companies:

1st Brigade,— included 4 Foot and 1 Horse company of Guards Artillery,—2 Battery, 3 Light, and 1 Pontoon company.

2nd Brigade: companies – 2 Battery, 2 Light, and 1 Horse.

3rd ——————— – 2 Battery, 3 Light, 1 Pontoon, and 1 Horse.

4th ——————— – 2 Battery, 3 Light, 1 Pontoon, and 1 Horse.

5th ——————— – 1 Battery, 2 Light, and 1 Horse.

6th ——————— – 2 Battery, 3 Light, and 1 Horse.

7th ——————— – 2 Battery, 3 Light, 1 Pontoon, and 1 Horse.

8th ——————— – 2 Battery, 2 Light, and 1 Horse.

9th ——————— – 2 Battery, 3 Light, and 1 Horse.

10th ——————— – 1 Battery, 3 Light, and 1 Horse.

11th ——————— – 2 Battery, 3 Light, 1 Pontoon, and 1 Horse.

12th ——————— – 3 Battery, 1 Light, 1 Pontoon, and 1 Horse.

13th ——————— – 1 Battery and 4 Light.

14th ——————— – 1 Battery, 2 Light, and 1 Pontoon.

15th ——————— – 3 Battery and 1 Horse.

Georgia Brigade: companies – 2 Battery and 3 Light.

Caucasus ——————— – 2 Battery, 2 Light, and 1 Pontoon.

Siberia   ——————— – 2 Battery and 2 Light (177).

**11 September 1806**– Five more brigades were established:

16th Brigade: companies – 1 Battery, 2 Light, and 1 Horse.

17th ——— ——— – 1 Battery, 2 Light, 1 Pontoon, and 1 Horse.

18th ——— ———— – 1 Battery, 2 Light, and 1 Horse.

St.-Petersburg Reserve Brigade: 6 Battery companies.

Kiev         ———— —— 6 Battery companies (178).

**11 February 1807**– The Moscow Reserve Brigade [*Moskovskaya Rezervnaya brigada*] was established, made up of 3 Battery companies and 2 Pontoon companies (179).

**16 February 1807**– The 19th and 20th Brigades were formed from the companies of the Georgia and Caucasus Brigades (180).

**1 June 1807**– All brigades were brought to the same number of companies: 2 Battery, 2 Light, 1 Horse, and 1 Pontoon, except for the 19th, 20th, and Siberia Brigades, which did not have Horse companies. Along with this an additional new brigade was formed, receiving the number 22nd, while the Army companies of the 1st Brigade formed the 21st Brigade (181).

**24 September 1807**– The 2nd Brigade was named the 3rd, and the 3rd—the 2nd (182).

**23 February 1808**– The Siberia Brigade was renamed the 23rd (183).

**1 October 1809**– The 7th Brigade was renamed the 9th, and the 9th—the 7th (184).

**18 September 1810**– The Pontoon companies of the 2nd, 8th, 17th, and 21st Field Brigades and of the Moscow Reserve Brigade were transferred to the Fortress Artillery [*Krepostnaya Artilleriya*] (185).

**31 January 1811**– *Artillery Recruit Depots [Artilleriiskiya Rekrutskiya Depo]* were established in Pskov, Smolensk, Starodub, and Konotop (186).

**7 February 1811**– The Starodub Depot was transferred to Bryansk, and the Konotop—to Glukhov (187).

**9 February 1811**– Officers of the Field Artillery [*Polevaya Artilleriya*] were granted seniority equal to that of Army officers one rank higher, up to Colonel (188).

**14 February 1811**– Artillery companies, which had been named for their commanders, were ordered to be numbered, and along with this, they were all used to form 26 new *Field [Polevaya]*, 10 *Reserve [Rezervnaya]*, and 4 *Replacement [Zapasnaya]* brigades with the following numbers of companies:

1st, 2nd, 3rd, 4th, 5th, 7th, 8th, 9th, 10th, 11th, 12th, 13th, 14th, 15th, 16th, 17th, 18th, 19th, 20th, 22nd, 23rd, 24th, and 26th *Field Brigades* — each of 1 Battery company and 2 Light companies.

6th and 21st *Field Brigades* — each of 1 Battery company and 1 Light company.

*25th Field Brigade,* of 1 Battery and 3 Light half-companies, located with the Marine regiments.

*1st Reserve Brigade:*——— 3 Horse, 2 Battery, and 2 Pontoon companies.

*2nd and 4th*——————— 3 Horse, 2 Battery, and 1 Pontoon companies.

*3rd*      —————————      4 Horse, 2 Battery, and 1 Pontoon companies.

*5th*      —————————      1 Battery, 1 Light, and 1 Pontoon company.

*6th and 7th*  —————————  2 Horse, 2 Battery, 1 Light, and 1 Pontoon company.

*8th*      —————————      1 Horse and 2 Battery companies.

*9th*      —————————      2 Battery companies.

*10th*     —————————      2 Battery and 1 Light company.

*1st, 2nd, 3rd, and 4th Replacement Brigades:* each of one Horse, one Battery, and four Pontoon companies (189).

**10 September 1811**– With all Army and Artillery Recruit Depots being used to organize two Reserve divisions and a Separate Reserve brigade, the Artillery Depots formed *Artillery brigades:* from the Pskov and Smolensk depots—for the *1st Reserve Division*, and from the Bryansk and Glukhov—for the *2nd* (190).

**15 October 1811**– A new Field brigade was established, made up of 1 Battery company and 2 Light companies (191).

**7 November 1811**– This brigade was named the *27th* Field Brigade (192).

**18 November 1811**– Artillery Recruit Depots were divided into companies:

Pskov and Smolensk depots — each into 6 Foot and 1 Horse company.

Bryansk ————— into 4 Foot and 3 Horse companies.

Glukhov ————— into 5 Foot and 2 Horse companies (193).

**22 November 1811**– With the renaming of Reserve divisions into corps, and their brigades into divisions, the brigades organized by the Artillery Depots received the title of *Artillery divisions [Artilleriiskiya divizii]:* from the Pskov and Smolensk depots—in the 1st Reserve Corps, and from the Bryansk and Glukhov depots—in the 2nd Reserve Corps (194).

**13 March 1812**– Active companies were formed at the Artillery Recruit Depots and assigned to Replacement brigades [*Zapasnyya brigady*]:

*To the 1st Replacement Brigade:*1 Battery, 4 Light, and 1 Horse company.

——*2nd* ———— ——— 1 Battery, 4 Light, and 1 Horse company.

—— *3rd* ————— ——— 3 Light and 3 Horse companies.

—— *4th* ————— ——— 1 Battery, 3 Light, and 3 Horse companies (195) .

**23 September 1814**– The establishments of Reserve and Replacement brigades were disbanded, and along with this it was ordered to have:

28 Foot brigades and 15 Horse companies – assigned to Armies; the first according to the number of Infantry divisions, and the second according to the number of Cavalry divisions.

2 Battery companies – for Georgia.

1 Battery company and 1 Light company – for the Orenburg Line.

22 Battery companies, including 4 without guns.

13½ Light companies, including 1½ companies with the Marine regiments and 4 companies without guns.

17 Horse companies, including 3 without guns.

24 Pontoon com.s, including 16 comp. without pontoons, distributed among fortresses, in place of garrisons, and at parks. The companies in the last four categories, numbering 76½, were not part of Artillery brigades and were not assigned to Army divisions, but rather were considered as extra pending further directions. Foot brigades from the 1st to the 20th [sic, should be 3rd – M.C.] inclusive were assigned as part of the 1st, 2nd, and 3rd Grenadier Divisions, and from the 4th through the 28th—as part of the Infantry divisions, so that the number of the Artillery brigade corresponded to the number of its Army division; Horse companies, however, were assigned to Cavalry divisions, one to each (196).

**1 October 1815**– The following changes took place:

It was ordered that the 1st, 4th, 5th, 6th, 7th, 8th, 9th, 10th, 12th, 13th, 14th, 15th, 18th, 21st, 22nd 24th, 26th, and 27th brigades each have 2 Battery and 2 Light companies.

In the 2nd, 3rd, 11th, 16th, 17th, 23rd, 25th, and 28th — 1 Battery and 3 Light companies.

In the 19th and 20th — 1 Battery and 2 Light companies.

With the 1st Cuirassier Division — 3 Horse companies.

With the 2nd and 3rd Cuirassier Divisions, 1st, 2nd, and 3rd Lancer Divisions, and 1st and 2nd Horse-Jäger Divisions—2 Horse companies each.

With the 1st, 2nd, and 3rd Hussar Divisions, 1st, 2nd, 3rd, and 4th Dragoon Divisions, and the Ukrainian Cossack Division—2 Horse and 1 Pontoon company each.

Not included in any brigade establishment, 3 Battery and 1 Light company for Georgia and the Orenburg Line remained in the same places as before, while 5 Battery, 4½ Light, and 16 Pontoon companies were left as extra pending further instructions (197).

**11 January 1816**– The 2nd, 3rd, 11th, 16th, 17th, 19th, 20th, 23rd, 25th, and 28th brigades were made the same as the other brigades, i.e. each of them was brought to an establishment of 2 Battery and 2 Light companies, and consequently 5 Battery, 5½ Light, and 16 Pontoon companies remained unassigned (198).

**26 July 1816**– Horse-Artillery companies were ordered to be two for every Cavalry division and have numbers from 1st to 30th inclusive (199).

**11 July 1817**– The 4th Brigade was renamed the 28th, and the latter—the 4th, and along with this the 27th and new 28th brigades were assigned to the Separate Lithuania Corps (200).

**18 April 1819**– The following changes took place in the Army's Foot Artillery establishment:

1) A new brigade was formed in the Separate Georgia Corps under the title *Georgia Grenadier Brigade [Gruzinskaya Grenaderskaya brigada]*, of 1 Battery and 2 Light companies.

2 ) The 1st, 2nd, and 3rd brigades were named the *1st, 2nd, and 3rd Grenadier Artillery Brigades [1-ya, 2-ya i 3-ya Grenaderskiya Artilleriiskiya brigady]*.

3) Each Grenadier brigade was designated to consist of two Battery companies No. № 1 and 2, one Light company № 3, one Park Battery company [*Parochnaya Batareinaya rota*] №4, and two Reserve Battery companies (without guns) No. No. 5 and 6, while each Field brigade—of one Battery company No. 1, two Light companies No. №2 and 3, one Park Battery [*Parochnaya Batareinaya*] company No. 4, and two Reserve Battery companies (without guns) No. No. 5 and 6. To form the new companies added by this reckoning, all the companies were to be used that had previously been extra. The Georgia Brigade consisted of three companies: a Battery company—№1, and Light companies—No. No. 2 and 3, while the 19th and 20th Field Brigades—of the same three companies as well as a Park Battery company No. 4.

4) Brigades were formed into divisions which were titled after the numbers and names of the corps with which they were located:

From the 1st, 2nd, and 3rd Grenadier Artillery Brigades: —*Grenadier Artillery Division*.

—— — 5 th, 14th, and 25th Artillery Brigades: — *1st Artillery Division*.

—— — 4th, 6th, and 17th ——— ———— *2nd Artillery Division*.

—— — 12th, 15th, and 26th ——— ———— *3rd Artillery Division.*
—— — 7th, 11th, and 24th  ——— ———— *4th Artillery Division.*
—— — 8th, 10th, and 23rd  ——— ———— *5th Artillery Division.*
—— — 13th and 16th   ——— ———— *6th Artillery Division.*
—— — 9th, 18th, and 22nd ——— ———— *7th Artillery Division.*
—— — 19th and 20th Georgia Grenadier Brigades: *Georgia Artillery Division.*
—— — 27th and 28th Artillery Brigades: *Lithuania Artillery Division.*

The 21st Artillery Brigade, stationed in Finland, did not belong to any division (201).

**20 March 1820–** The following changes took place in regard to the numbers assigned to Field Artillery brigades:

25th Brigade, in the 1st Army, with the 1st Infantry Corps, named . . 1.
5th ——————— ——————— ——————— . . 2.
14th ——————— ——————— ——————— . . 3.
4th ———— ———— — 2nd ——— —— kept No. 4.
17th ———— ———— ————— named . . 5.
6th ———— ———— ———— —— kept No. 6.
12th ———— ———— — 3rd ——— —— named . . 7.
15th ————— ————— ————— . . 8.
26th ————— ————— ————— . . 9.
7th ———— ———— — 4th ——— —— . . 10.
11th ———— ———— ————— kept No. 11.
24th ———— ———— ———— named . . 12.
8th ———— ———— — 5th ——— —— . . 13.
23rd ————— ————— ————— . . 14.
10th ————— ————— ————— . . 15.
16th ————— 2nd ——— — 6th ——— —— kept № 16.
13th ———— ———— ———— named . . 17.
18th ———— ———— — 7th ——— —— kept No. 18.
22nd ———— ———— ———— named . . 19.
9th ————— ————— ————— . . 20.
20th ————— with the Separate Georgia Corps ———— . . 21.
19th ———————————— ———— . . 22.
23rd ————————— Finland ————————— kept No. 23.
27th ————————— Lithuania ————————— named . . 24.
28th ————————————— ———— . . 25 [202].

**21 October 1820–** The Georgia Artillery Division and the Georgia Grenadier Artillery Brigade were ordered to be named the *Caucasus* division and brigade (203).

**20 April 1822–** Pontoon companies, which were in Infantry Corps, one each, to the number of eight, and in the three Hussar divisions, four Dragoon divisions, and the Ukrainian Lancer Division, were removed to the Engineer Department [*Inzhenernoe vedomstvo*], where they formed Pontoon sections [*Pontonnyya otdeleniya*] in the Sapper and Pioneer battalions.

After all these changes, by 1826 the Army Artillery consisted of the following brigades:

1st, 2nd, and 3rd Grenadier Artillery Brigades [*Grenaderskiya Artilleriiskiya brigady*], each of two Battery companies №№ 1 and 2, Light company № 3, Park Battery company № 4, and Reserve Batteries №№ 5 and 6.

Caucasus Grenadier Artillery Brigade [*Kavkazskaya Grenaderskaya Artilleriiskaya brigada*], of Battery company № 1 and Light companies №№ 2 and 3.

1st, 2nd, 3rd, 4th, 5th, 6th, 7th, 8th, 9th, 10th, 11th, 12th, 13th, 14th, 15th, 16th, 17th, 18th, 19th, and 20th Field Artillery Brigades [*Polevyya Artilleriiskiya brigady*], each of a Battery company №1, Light companies №№ 2 and 3, Park Battery company № 4, and Reserve Batteries №№ 5 and 6.

21st, 22nd, and 23rd Field Artillery Brigades, each of Battery company №1, Light companies №№ 2 and 3, Park Battery company № 4, and Reserve Battery № 5.

24th and 25th Field Artillery Brigades, each of Battery company №1, Light companies №№ 2 and 3, and Park Battery company № 4.

Horse companies kept their numbers, from 1st through 30th inclusive (204).

# ARMY SAPPERS AND PIONEERS

**15 June 1803** – The Pioneer Regiment [*Pionernyi polk*] was ordered to consist of two battalions, and the battalions—of one Miner [*Minernaya*] and three Pioneer companies (205).

**27 July 1803** – This regiment was divided into two: *the 1st and 2nd Pioneers* (206).

**22 March 1806** – These regiments were ordered to consist of three battalions, and the battalions—of one company of Miner-Sappers [*Miner-Sapery*] and three companies of Pioneers (207).

**24 October 1810** – These battalions were ordered to consist of one company of Miners, one Sapper company, and two companies of Pioneers (208).

**9 December 1810** – These battalions were ordered to consist of, as before, one Miner and three Pioneer companies, with each Miner company being one-half Miner and the other half Sapper (209).

**30 March 1811** – Officers of Pioneer regiments were granted the same privileges as similar Army ranks, up to Lieutenant Colonel (210).

**20 December 1812** – It was ordered to form five new Pioneer battalions: in Riga and Kiev—one each, in Viborg—two, and in Sveaborg—one (211).

**27 December 1812** – A *Sapper Regiment [Sapernyi polk]* was formed from the Miners and Sappers in the Pioneer battalions, while the Pioneer companies were used to form the *1st* and *2nd Pioneer Regiments*. All these regiments were of three battalions, and the battalions were divided into four companies (212).

**11 January 1816** – From the Sapper Regiment and both Pioneer regiments were formed the following battalions: *Sapper battalions*– of two Sapper and two Miner companies, and *Miner battalions*– of one Sapper and three Pioneer companies:

    *1st Sapper Battalion*—  for the Grenadier Corps.

    *2nd* ——————— — Reserves.

    *1st Pioneer* ——— — 1st Infantry Corps.

    *2nd* ——————— — 2nd ——— ——

    *3rd* ——————— — 3rd ——— ——

    *4th* ——————— — 4th ——— ——

    *5th* ——————— — 5th ——— ——

    *6th* ——————— — 6th ——— ——

    *7th* ——————— — 2nd Army [213].

**28 March 1816** – The *Pioneer company for the Georgian Military Road [Pionernaya rota pri Voenno-Gruzinskoi doroge]* was established (214).

**26 May 1817** – A Pioneer company was established for the *Separate Georgia Corps* (215).

**13 September 1818** – Both these companies were directed to be called the *8th Pioneer Battalion* (216).

**20 April 1822** – The 1st Sapper Battalion was named the *Sapper Battalion of the Grenadier Corps*. Along with this, it was designated to be settled in Novgorod Province, for which villages were transferred under the name *Military Settlement District of the Sapper Battalion of the Grenadier Corps [Okrug Voennago Poseleniya Sapernago bataliona Grenaderskago Korpusa]*. In these villages, from part of their original inhabitants and from personnel of Sapper and Pioneer battalions who entered service from Pskov or Novgorod provinces, were formed two companies called the *Settled Companies [Poselennyya roty]* of the Sapper Battalion of the Grenadier Corps, and consequently the battalion received an establishment of four active and two settled companies (217).

**21 April 1822** – The 2nd Sapper Battalion was designated for training non-commissioned officers, drummers, and buglers for Sapper and Pioneer battalions, as well as draftsmen [*konduktora*] for the Engineer Corps [*Inzhenernyi Korpus*], and was named the *Instructional Sapper Battalion [Uchebnyi Sapernyi batalion]* (218).

**22 April 1822** – The Sapper Battalion and first seven Pioneer battalions were directed to have 42 pontoons each, which came from the Pontoon companies in the Artillery (219).

**2 August 1822** – The *1st Horse-Pioneer Squadron [1-i Konno-Pionernyi eskadron]* was established (220).

**21 February 1823** – From the pontoons of the Separate Lithuania Corps it was ordered to form, for this corps, a *Pioneer Battalion* (221).

**14 August 1823** – This battalion was named the *9th Pioneers* (222).

**19 September 1823** – This battalion was ordered to be named the *Lithuania Pioneers [Litovskii Pionernyi]* (223).

At the time Emperor Alexander i passed away, there were ten Army Sapper and Pioneer battalions assigned to corps:

Sapper Battalion - for the Grenadier Corps.
1st Pioneer Bn. — — 1st Infantry Corps.
2nd ————— — 2nd ——— ——
3rd ————— — 3rd ———— ——
4th ————— — 4th ———— ——
5th ————— — 5th ———— ——
6th ————— — 6th ———— ——
7th ————— — 7th ———— ——
8th ————— — Separate Caucasus Corps.
Lithuania Pioneer Bn. ——— Lithuania ——

The Instructional Sapper Battalion and the 1st Horse-Pioneer Squadron were with the Guards Corps, while the Settled companies of the Sapper Battalion were in the Separate Corps of Military Settlements (224).

# ARMY TRAIN

**2 May 1819** – In order to provide the forces with more means to transport provisions while on the march, and to preserve the treasury from excessive expenditures during peacetime, in each of the Infantry Corps—consisting of three Infantry, one Cavalry, and one Artillery division, one Sapper or Pioneer battalion, and one Pontoon company—it was decided to establish *Train battalions [Furshtatskie bataliony]*, each of six companies, in place of the existing regimental trains [*polkovye obozy*]. One of these companies, or 16 wagons [*fury*], was prescribed for the two active battalions of each Infantry regiment; 3/4 of a company – for the six active squadrons of a Cavalry regiment; 9 wagons – for one Foot Artillery brigade; 6 wagons – for two Horse-Artillery companies; 1/2 of a company – for a Sapper or Pioneer battalion; and 3 wagons – for a Pontoon company, i.e. a total of four battalions or one *brigade* for each corps. As a first step, such brigades were established for the 1st, 2nd, 3rd, and 4th Infantry Corps (225).

**25 October 1819**– These brigades were directed to be named: the brigade assigned to the 1st Infantry Corps—*1st Train Brigade [1-ya Furshtatskaya brigada]*, to the 2nd—*2nd*, to the 3rd—*3rd*, and to the 4th—*4th*, while the battalions of each brigade were: 1st, 2nd, 3rd, and 4th, according to the seniority of the division within the corps (226).

**23 May 1820**– It was ordered that every Settled battalion have a *Settled Train company [Poselennaya Furshtatskaya rota]* of four sections [*otdeleniya*]: the 1st or settled [*poselennoe*], the 2nd or active [*deistvuyushchee*], the 3rd or non-combatant ranks' [*nestroevykh chinov*], and the 4th or reserve [*rezervnoe*] (227).

**10 September 1820**– Another four Train brigades were ordered to be formed for the Grenadier Corps, 5th Infantry Corps, and 2nd, 3rd, 4th, and 5th Reserve Cavalry Corps (228).

**1 October 1820**– The same type of brigade was established for the Separate Lithuania Corps (229).

**20 November 1820**– The four Train brigades established on 10 September were named:

5th Train Brigade — for the 5th Infantry Corps.
6th ————— — Grenadier Corps .
7th ————— — 2nd and 3rdReserve Cavalry Corps.
8th ————— — 4th and 5thCorps.

Of the battalions of the 7th and 8th brigades, one was assigned to each Cavalry division, along with its two constituent Horse-Artillery companies, of the 2nd, 3rd, 4th, and 5th Reserve Corps (230).

**2 February 1822**– The 6th Train Brigade was named the *Grenadier Train Brigade [Grenaderskaya Furshtatskaya brigada]* (231).

**17 April 1822**– The Train brigade of the Separate Lithuania Corps was named the *Lithuania Train Brigade [Litovskaya Furshtatskaya brigada]* (232), and consequently there were nine Train brigades in all: the Grenadier, 1st, 2nd, 3rd, 4th, 5th, 6th, 7th, 8th, and Lithuania.

# GARRISON REGIMENTS AND BATTALIONS

**17 April 1801**– Colonel Koshelev's Garrison Regiment (in Akhtiar, or Sevastopol, Nikolaev, and Perekop) was named *Major General Prince Vyazemskii's Garrison Regiment [Garnizonnyi General-Maiora Knyazya Vyazemskago polk]* (233). [Akhtiar was the name of the original Tatar village on the site where Sevastopol was founded in 1783. – M.C.]

**19 April 1801**– Major General Graf Liven 3rd's Garrison Regiment (in Astrakhan, Tsaritsyn, and Simbirsk) was named *Major General Zavalishin's Garrison Regiment [Garnizonnyi General-Maiora Zavalishina polk]* (234).

**3 July 1801**– All Garrison regiments and battalions, which until then were named after their Regimental Colonels [*Shefy*], were named, as before, after the places where they were stationed:

### a.) Finland Inpectorate:

Essen 3rd's Regiment, two battalions, in Viborg — as the *Vyborgskii Garnizonnyi polk*.

—— —— Regiment, two battalions, in Fredrikshamn — as the *Fridrikhsgamskii Garnizonnyi polk*.

Bolotnikov's Regiment, three battalions, in Rochensalm — as the *Rochensalmskii Garnizonnyi polk*.

Plutalov's Regiment: one battalion, in Villmanstrand — as the *Vilmanstrandskii Garnizonnyi batalion*.

———— Kexholm — as the *Keksgolmskii Garnizonnyi batalion*.

———— Nyslott — as the *Neishlotskii Garnizonnyi batalion*.

### b.) St.-Petersburg Inpectorate:

Ukolov's Regiment, of four battalions, in Kronstadt — as the *Kronshtadtskii Garnizonnyi polk*.

Vyrubov's Regiment: one battalion, in Narva — as the *Narvskii Garnizonnyi batalion*.

———— Novgorod — as the *Novgorodskii Garnizonnyi batalion*.

———— Pskov — as the *Pskovskii Garnizonnyi batalion*.

Plutalov's Regiment, one battalion, in Schlüsselburg — as the *Shlisselburg Garnizonnyi batalion*.

### c.) Livonia Inpectorate:

Bulgakov's Regiment, of four battalions, in Riga — as the *Rizhskii Garnizonnyi polk*.

Balashev's Regiment, of three battalions, in Reval — as the *Revelskii Garnizonnyi polk*.

———— Regiment, one battalion, in Pernau — as the *Pernovskii Garnizonnyi batalion*.

Prince Gika's Regiment, of three battalions, in Dünamünde — as the *Dinamindskii Garnizonnyi batalion*.

Bolotnikov's Regiment, one battalion, in Arensburg — as the *Arensburgskii Garnizonnyi batalion*.

### d.) Dnieper Inpectorate:

Masse's Regiment, two battalions, in Kherson — as the *Khersonskii Garnizonnyi polk*.

Prince Vyazemskii's Regiment, one battalion, designated for transfer from Nikolaev to Ochakov and Kinburn — as the *Ochakovskii Garnizonnyi batalion*.

### e.) Crimea Inpectorate:

Prince Vyazemskii's Regiment, two battalions, in Akhtiar — as the *Akhtiarskii Garnizonnyi polk*.

——— ———— ——— one battalion, in Perekop — as the *Perekopskii Garnizonnyi batalion*.

### f.) Caucasus Inpectorate:

Zavalishin's Regiment, two battalions, in Astrakhan — as the *Astrakhanskii Garnizonnyi polk*.

———— ———— one battalion, in Tsaritsyn — as the *Tsaritsynskii Garnizonnyi batalion*.

Olvintsev's Regiment, two battalions, in the St.-Dimitrii Fortress — as the *Dimitrievskii Garnizonnyi polk*.

———— ———— one battalion, in Azov — as the *Azovskii Garnizonnyi batalion*.

———— ———— one battalion, in Taganrog — as the *Taganrogskii Garnizonnyi batalion*.

### g.) Smolensk Inpectorate:

Prince Gika's Regiment: one battalion, in Smolensk — as the *Smolenskii Garnizonnyi batalion*.

—— —— —— ———— —— Vitebsk — as the *Vitebskii Garnizonnyi batalion*.

—— —— —— ———— —— Mogilev — as the *Mogilevskii Garnizonnyi batalion*.

### h.) Kiev Inpectorate:

Masse's Regiment, two battalions, in Kiev — as the *Kievskii Garnizonnyi polk*.

### i.) Moscow Inpectorate:

Reichenberg's Regiment, of four battalions, in Moscow — as the *Moskovskii Garnizonnyi polk*.

Vyrubov's Regiment, one battalion, in Tver — as the *Tverskii Garnizonnyi batalion*.

Lebedev's Regiment: one battalion, in Tambov — as the *Tambovskii Garnizonnyi batalion*.

———— ——— ———————— Voronezh — as the *Voronezhskii Garnizonnyi batalion*.

Korf's Regiment, one battalion, in Saratov — as the *Saratovskii Garnizonnyi batalion*.

Graf Liven 1st's Regiment: one battalion, in Vladimir — as the *Vladimirskii Garnizonnyi batalion*.

———————— ——— ———— — Nizhnii-Novgorod — as the *Nizhegorodskii Garnizonnyi batalion*.

———————— ——— two battalions — Archangel — as the *Arkhangelogorodskii Garnizonnyi polk*.

### k.) **Orenburg Inpectorate:**

Zavalishin's Regiment, one battalion, in Simbirsk — as the *Simbirskii Garnizonnyi batalion.*

Pushchin 1st's Regiment, two battalions, in Kazan — as the *Kazanskii Garnizonnyi polk.*

Lebedev's Regiment, two battalions, in Orenburg — as the *Orenburgskii Garnizonnyi polk.*

Korf's Regiment: one battalion, in Orsk Fortress — as the *Orskii Garnizonnyi batalion.*

——————— —— ——— — Kizilsk Fortress — as the *Kizilskii Garnizonnyi batalion.*

——————— —— ——— — Zverinogolovsk Fortress — as the *Zverinogolovskii Garnizonnyi batalion.*

Borshchov's Regiment, one battalion, in Verkhne-Uralsk Fortress — as the *Verkhneuralskii Garnizonnyi batalion.*

——————— ——— one battalion, in Troitsk Fortress — as the *Troitskii Garnizonnyi batalion.*

### l.) **Siberia Inpectorate:**

Pushchin 1st's Regiment, two battalions, in Tobolsk — as the *Tobolskii Garnizonnyi polk.*

Retyunskii's Regiment, one battalion, in Omsk — as the *Omskii Garnizonnyi batalion.*

——————— ——— one battalion, in Zhelezinka and Yamyshevo fortresses— as the *Zhelezninskii Garnizonnyi batalion.*

——————— ——— one battalion, in Biisk and Kizilsk fortresses — as the *Biiskii Garnizonnyi batalion.*

Boritsov's Regiment, one battalion, in St.-Peter Fortress — as the *Petrovskii Garnizonnyi batalion.*

——————— ——— one battalion, in Semipalatinsk Fortress — as the *Semipalatinskii Garnizonnyi batalion.*

Letstsano's Regiment, two battalions, Retyunskii's Regiment, one battalion, transferred from Tomsk— in Irkutsk and Nerchinskas the *Irkutskii Garnizonnyi polk.*

——————— ——— two battalions, in Selenginsk — as the *Selenginskii Garnizonnyi polk.*

Somov's Regiment, of one battalion, in Kamchatka — as the *Kamchatskii Garnizonnyi batalion.*

Along with this, from the four Grenadier companies detached from Retyunskii's Regiment and stationed at Tara, there was established a separate Garrison battalion under the name *Tarskii* (235).

**17 August 1801**– There were established: the *Kizlyarskii Garnizonnyi polk* and *Mozdokskii Garnizonnyi batalion*; both were on an internal establishment, and a 3rd battalion was added to the Astrakhan Garrison Regiment (236).

**19 March 1802**– The Archangel Garrison Regiment was brought to a three-battalion establishment (237).

**30 April 1802**– All Garrison battalions were ordered to be made up of four Combatant [*Stroevaya*], or Musketeer [*Mushketerskaya*], companies, and those that were on the internal establishment were to each have an additional single Invalid company (238).

**14 August 1803**– Garrison battalions were established: the *Mitavskii* [Mitau] and *Grodnenskii* [Grodno], for the formation of which one battalion each was detached from the Riga and Reval Garrison Regiments (239).

**9 November 1803**– The Kamchatka Garrison Battalion was ordered to consist of five Land [*Sukhoputnaya*] companies and one Marine [*Morskaya*] company (240).

**16 November 1803**– The Tara Garrison Battalion was transferred to Tomsk and named the *Tomskii* (241).

**4 January 1804**– New Garrison battalions were established: the *Vilenskii [Vilna], Minskii,Yekaterinoslavskii [Yekaterinoslavl],Vologodskii [Vologda],Velikoustyuzhskii [Velikii-Ustyug],Ufimskii [Ufa],Vyatskii [Vyatka],*and *Vladikavkazskii.* The first was on a field establishment [*polevoe polozhenie*] and the rest on the internal establishment [*vnutrennee polozhenie*], with assignments to the following Inspectorates:

Vilna and Minsk — in Lithuania Inspectorate.

Yekaterinoslavl — in Kiev Inspectorate.

Vologda and Velikie-Luki [sic, should be Velikii-Ustyug – M.C.] — in Moscow Inspectorate.

Ufa and Vyatka — in Orenburg Inspectorate.

Vladikavkaz — in Caucasus Inspectorate.

**7 April 1804**– The Vladikavkaz Garrison Battalion was ordered to be maintained at a field establishment (243).

**28 November 1804**– In order to maintain Garrisons in the fortifications of the Orenburg Line, four Garrison battalions were established under the names *1st,2nd,3rd,* and *4th Orenburg Line Battalions [Orenburgskie Lineinye bataliony]*, and to the Garrison battalion already at the Vladikavkaz Fortress there was added an additional newly formed battalion, which together with the original one formed the *Vladikavkaz Garrison Regiment* (244).

**8 June 1805**– The Yekaterinoslavl Garrison Battalion was reassigned to the Crimea Inspectorate (245).

**7 February 1806**– The *Penzinskii [Penza] Garnizonnyi batalion* was established (246).

**16 June 1806–** The following Garrison regiments and battalions were assigned to the newly formed divisions:

Schlüsselburg and Narva battalions —— to the 1st Division.

Riga and Reval regiments and Pernau, Dünamünde, Arensburg, and Mitau battalions —— to the 2nd Division.

Vilna, Grodno, and Minsk battalions —— to the 4th Division.

Vitebsk and Mogilev battalions —— to the 5th Division.

Kiev Regiment ——to the 10th Division.

Kherson and Akhtiar regiments and Perekop, Ochakov, and Yekaternislavl battalions ——to the 13th Division.

Novgorod and Pskov battalions —— to the 14th Division[247].

**5 October 1806–** One battalion of the Akhtiar Garrison Regiment was used in forming the Kura Musketeer Regiment, and consequently there remained only one battalion in Akhtiar, or Sevastopol, receiving the name *Akhtiarskii Garnizonnyi bat.*(248).

**15 November 1806–** The Garrisons which were in the Moscow Inspectorate were assigned to the 18th Division (249).

**21 May 1807–** The Mozdok Garrison Battalion was ordered to be maintained at a field establishment (250).

**31 December 1807–** The Kizlyar Garrison Regiment was ordered to be maintained at a field establishment (251).

**5 February 1808–** The Orenburg and Siberia inspectorates were ordered to be titled *divisions [divizii]*: the first—the *23rd*, and the second—the *24th* (252).

**22 October 1809–** The Pskov Garrison Battalion, because of its transfer to Gangut Fortress, was named the *Gangutskii Garnizonnyi batalion*. And using one battalion from the Fredrikshamn Garrison Regiment as well as the Villmanstrand, Kexholm, Schlüsselburg, and Novgorod Garrison Battalions, there were formed *Garrison regiments*: the four-battalion *Sveaborgskii* and the three-battalion *Alandskii*; the battalion of the Fredrikshamn Garrison Regiment left in that city was named the *Fridrikhsgamskii Garnizonnyi batalion* (253).

**21 October 1809–** An additional battalion was established for the Omsk Garrison Battalion, which, along with the new battalion, was ordered to be called the *Omskii Garnizonnyi polk* (254).

**10 January 1810–** The Tver Garrison battalion was ordered to be maintained at a field establishment (255).

**22 January 1810–** The *Potiiskii [Poti] Garnizonnyi batalion* was established (256).

**23 August 1810–** The Minsk Garrison Battalion was named the *Bobruiskii*, and the Mitau—the *Dinaburgskii [Dünaburg]* (257).

**26 August 1810–** One of the battalions of the Irkutsk Garrison Regiment was detached to the Omsk Garrison Regiment, bringing the latter to three battalions, while the former was left with a two-battalion establishment (258).

**19 October 1810–** The Grodno Garrison Battalion was named the *Kyumenegorodskii Garnizonnyi batalion*, the Nizhnii-Novgorod—*Khotinskii*, the Yekaterinoslavl—*Akkermanskii*, the Vladimir—*Kerch-Yenikolskii [Kerch-Yenikale]*, one battalion of the Kherson Garrison Regiment—*Benderskii [Bender or Bendery]*, and one battalion of the Kizlyar Garrison Regiment—*Derbentskii*. The Saratov Garrison Battalion was used for part of the Kizlyar Garrison Regiment, replacing the battalion transferred to Derbent. The battalion of the Kherson Garrison Regiment left in that city was named the *Khersonskii Garnizonnyi batalion*. The Mogilev Garrison Battalion was joined to the Kiev Garrison Regiment, which in this way was then made up of three battalions. The third battalion of the Astrakhan Garrison Regiment, along with the Penza Garrison Battalion, formed the *Bakinskii [Baku] Garnizonnyi polk*, and the *Anapskii [Anapa] Garnizonnyi polk* was formed from the Azov and Vitebsk Garrison Battalions (259).

**3 November 1810–** It was directed that the Garrisons of the Orenburg Line compose the *25th Division*, and the Garrisons of the Siberia Line—the *26th* (260).

**17 January 1811–** The Viborg, Aland, Sveaborg, Rochensalm, Kronstadt, Reval, Riga, Kiev, and Dmitrievsk Garrison Regiments, as well as the Nyslott, Fredrikshamn, Gangeut [sic, alternative spelling of Gangut – M.C.], Tver, Narva, Dünamünde, Vilna, Dünaburg, Kyumenegorod, Bobruisk, Kherson, Ochakov, Poti, Tsaritsyn, Tambov, one battalion of the Baku, Kerch-Yenikale, Taganrog, Akkerman, Akhtiar, Kiev, Smolensk, Khotin, Bender, Perekop, and Voronezh Garrison Battalions, totaling 52 battalions, were disbanded. It was in this way that three companies from each battalion, picked from the best personnel, were used to form the ten new Musketeer and three new Jäger regiments*. Twelve companies formed new four-company Garrison battalions: *1st* and *2nd Crimea* and a new *Poti*, while forty companies were distributed to the same number of provincial capitals [*gubernskie goroda*] to there form the basis, in conjunction with state provincial companies [*shtatnyya gubernskiya roty*], of two-company *Internal Garrison [Vnutrennye Garnizonnye]*, or *Provincial [Gubernskie], half-battalions [polubataliony]*. These cities were as follows:

*Kuopio, Novgorod, Smolensk, Kaluga, Vologda, Kostroma, Nizhnii-Novgorod, Yaroslavl, Vladimir, Orel, Viborg, Peterburg, Grodno, Petrozavodsk, Penza, Pskov, Kursk, Chernigov, Perm, Tula, Ryazan, Vitebsk, Mogilev, Riga, Mitau, Minsk, Bialystok, Zhitomir, Vilna, Poltava, Kamenets-Podolskii, Kharkov, Voronezh, Tambov, Saratov, Georgievsk, Tver*, and *Kiev*.

After this, only the following of the former garrisons remained not disbanded: the *Moscow, Archangel, Kazan,Orenburg, Tobolsk, Omsk, Irkutsk, Astrakhan, Kizlyar,* and *Anapa regiments,* and the *Arensburg, Simbirsk, Vyatka, Kizilsk, Zverinogolovsk, Verkhne-Uralsk, Troitsk, Ufa, Biisk, Petrovsk, Zhelezinka, Semipalatinsk, Tomsk, Baku, Derbent,* and *Mozdok* battalions (261).
*Mentioned above, in the chapter: *Army Infantry*.

**14 March 1811**– The 1st Crimea Garrison Battalion was named the *Khersonskii,* and the 2nd Crimea—the *Tavricheskii [Taurica].* Also, the three-company *Yekaterinoslavl Internal Garrison Half-Battalion [Yekaterinoslavskii Vnutrennii Garnizonnyi polubatalion]* was established. Along with this, confirmation was given to the following distribution of garrisons of the *Internal Guard [Vnutrennyaya Strazha]* to regions *[okruga]* and brigades:

 1st Region, 1st Brigade: Petrozavodsk, Kuopio, and Viborg half-battalions.
   —— 2nd —— St.-Petersburg and Novgorod half-battalions.
   —— 3rd —— Reval and Riga half-battalions.
 2nd —— 1st —— Tver and Pskov half-battalions.
   —— 2nd —— Vitebsk and Mitau half-battalions.
 3rd —— 1st —— Kaluga, Smolensk, and Mogilev half-battalions.
   —— 2nd —— Minsk and Vilna half-battalions.
 4th —— 1st —— Tula, Orel, and Chernigov half-battalions.
   —— 2nd —— Grodno and Bialystok half-battalions.
 5th —— 1st —— Kursk, Kharkov, and Poltava half-battalions.
   —— 2nd —— Kiev and Zhitomir half-battalions.
 6th —— 1st —— Yekaterinoslavl Half-Battalion and Taurica and Kherson battalions.
   —— 2nd —— Kamenets-Podolskii and Tarnopol half-battalions.
 7th —— 1st —— Vologda and Kostroma half-battalions.
   —— 2nd —— Vyatka Battalion and Perm Half-Battalion.
   —— 3rd —— Kazan Regiment and Nizhnii-Novgorod Half-Battalion.
   —— 4th —— Vladimir and Yaroslavl half-battalions.
 8th —— 1st —— Ryazan, Tambov, and Penza half-battalions.
   —— 2nd —— Simbirsk and Ufa battalions.
   —— 3rd —— Saratov and Voronezh half-battalions.

Garrison regiments and battalions: in Archangel, Arensburg, Moscow, Astrakhan, in Georgia, on the Caucasian and Orenburg lines, and in Siberia, did not come under the Internal Guard, but rather remained, as before, under the authority of local Commandants and Military Governors (262).

**10 March 1811**– The Vologda and Velikii-Ustyug Garrison Battalions were used for the Moscow Garrison Regiment; the Simbirsk and Ufa Garrison Battalions were brought from a four-company establishment to three companies; and a new, four-company, *Uralskii Garnizonnyi batalion* was established (263).

**27 March 1811**– It was ordered to bring the half-battalions of the Internal Guard to a three-company establishment, as far as possible, and in carrying this out, to submit them for naming as *battalions.* Consequently, at this time the following were named *battalions:* the Novgorod, Smolensk, Kaluga, Vologda, Nizhnii-Novgorod, Yaroslavl, Vladimir, Grodno, Chernigov, Perm, Tula, Ryazan, Vitebsk, Mogilev, Riga, Bialystok, Zhitomir, Tver, and Georgievsk, this last being assigned to the 3rd Brigade of the 8th Region (264).

**15 July 1811**– The Pskov *Internal* Half-Battalion, with the formation of a third company for it, was named the *Pskov Internal Garrison Battalion [Pskovskii Vnutrennii Garnizonnyi batalion]* (265).

**18 September 1811**– The Viborg Half-Battalion, with the formation of a third company for it, was named the *Viborg Internal Garrison Battalion* (266).

**24 September 1811**– The St.-Petersburg Half-Battalion, with the formation of a third company for it, was named the *St.-Petersburg Internal Garrison Battalion* (267).

**6 November 1811**– The Garrisons of the Orenburg Territory *[Orenburgskii krai]* were to compose the *28th* Infantry Division, and the Siberia Garrisons—the *27th* (268).

**4 December 1811**– The Kuopio and Kamenets-Podolskii half-battalions, with the formation of third companies for them, were named the *Kuopio and Kamenets-Podolskii Internal Garrison Battalions* (269).

**25 December 1811**– The Voronezh, Penza, Tambov, and Saratov half-battalions, with the formation of third companies for them, were named the *Voronezh, Penza, Tambov,* and *Saratov Internal Garrison Battalions* (270).

**10 January 1812**– The Kursk, Reval, and Kiev half-battalions, with the formation of third companies for them, were named the *Kursk, Reval,* and *Kiev Internal Garrison Battalions* (271).

**13 January 1812**– The Kostroma Half-Battalion, with the formation of a third company for it, was named the *Kostroma Internal Garrison Battalion* (272).

**25 January 1812**– The Vilna and Mitau half-battalions, with the formation of third companies for them, were named the *Vilna* and *Mitau Internal Garrison Battalions* (273).

**30 January 1812**– The Petrozavodsk Half-Battalion, with the formation of a third company for it, was named the *Petrozavodsk Internal Garrison Battalion* (274).

**5 February 1812**– The Minsk Half-Battalion, with the formation of a third company for it, was named the *Minsk Internal Garrison Battalion* (275).

**12 March 1812**– The Poltava Half-Battalion, with the formation of a third company for it, was named the *Poltava Internal Garrison Battalion* (276).

**9 April 1812**– The Kamchatka Garrison Battalion was disbanded (277).

**13 August 1812**– The Yekaterinoslavl Half-Battalion, with the formation of a third company for it, was named the *Yekaterinoslav Internal Garrison Battalion* (278).

**1 November 1812**– The Uralsk Garrison Battalion was reassigned to a field establishment (279).

**20 November 1812**– The Tarnopol Half-Battalion, with the formation of a third company for it, was named the *Tarnopol Internal Garrison Battalion* (280).

**13 January 1813**– The Orel Half-Battalion, with the formation of a third company for it, was named the *Orel Internal Garrison Battalion* (281).

**9 March 1813**– The Kharkov Half-Battalion, with the formation of a third company for it, was named the *Kharkov Internal Garrison Battalion* (282).

**11 March 1813**– The Moscow Garrison Regiment, after the removal of the greater part of its personnel to make up the new Borodino and Tarutino Infantry Regiments, was reformed into a *battalion* under the name *Moscow Internal Garrison Battalion* (283), and in this same year, due to the lack of troops to maintain a garrision in the fortress of Lenkoran, the *Temporary Lenkoran Battalion [Vremennyi Lenkoranskii batalion]* was established there (284).

**10 January 1814**– The *Kishinev Internal Garrison Battalion* was established, made up of three companies (285).

**1 February 1814**– The Vladikavkaz Garrison Regiment was brought to a strength of three battalions (286).

**28 May 1815**– With the cession to Austria of part of Galicia, according to the Congress of Vienna, the Tarnopol Internal Garrison Battalion which was there was disbanded (287).

**3 February 1816**– The Archangel Garrision Regiment was reassigned to a field establishment (288).

**12 February 1816**– The *Guriiskii [Guria] Garnizonnyi polk* was formed from the Poti Garrison Battalion and the battalion of the Kizlyar Garrison Regiment which had been transferred to Guria to the fortress of St. Nicholas, and the battalion left at Kizlyar was named the *Kizlyarskii Garnizonnyi batalion* (289).

**30 March 1816**– The Internal Guard [*Vnutrenyaya Strazha*] was ordered to be named the *Separate Corps of the Internal Guard [Otdelnyi Korpus Vnutrennei Strazhi]* (290).

**28 June 1816**– The Tiflis *Internal Garrison Battalion*, made up of three companies, was established and assigned to the 4th Brigade of the VIII Region of the Separate Corps of the Internal Guard (291).

**14 July 1816**– Battalions of the Separate Corps of the Internal Guard were ordered to be named *Garrison battalions*, and not to be called provincial [*gubernskii*] (292).

**17 August 1816**– The Kazan and Archangel Garrison Regiments and the Arensburg Garrison Battalion were assigned to the Separate Corps of the Internal Guard, keeping their field establishment, as before (293).

**4 September 1816**– The Tobolsk Garrison Regiment was divided into separate Garrison battalions: the *Tobolskii* and *Tomskii*, and the former Tomsk Garrison Battalion was renamed the *Ust-Kamenogorskii*. With this, these three battalions and the Irkutsk Garrison Regiment were charged with responsibility for the Internal Guard in Siberia (294).

**2 October 1816**– The Novgorod Internal Garrison Battalion was brought to an establishment of four companies (295).

**18 December 1816**– The Garrisons of the Orenburg Territory, or the 29th Infantry Division, and the Siberia Garrisons, or the 30th Infantry Division, came under the *Orenburg* and *Siberia Separate Corps [Orenburgskii i Sibirskii Otdelnye Korpusa]* (296).

**7 January 1817**– All battalions of the Internal Guard were directed to consist of four companies (297).

**9 April 1817**– The Anapa Garrison Regiment was named the *Tamanskii* (298).

**13 May 1817**– The Temporary Lenkoran Battalion was disbanded (299).

**20 February 1818**– A new listing of Internal Guard regiments and battalions in regions and brigades was confirmed:

1st Region, 1st Brigade: Mitau and Riga battalions.

———— 2nd —— Reval, Arensburg, and Pskov battalions.

2nd ———— 1st —— Vitebsk and Smolensk battalions.

———— 2nd —— Mogilev and Kaluga battalions.

3rd ———— 1st —— Chernigov and Kiev battalions.

———— 2nd —— Poltava, Kharkov, and Kursk battalions.

4th ———— 1st —— Kishinev and Kherson battalions.

———— 2nd —— Yekaterinoslavl and Taurica battalions.

5th ———— 1st —— Viborg and Kuopio battalions.

———— 2nd —— Archangel Regiment.

———— 3rd —— Petrozavodsk and Vologda battalions.

6th ———— 1st —— St.-Petersburg and Novgorod battalions.

———— 2nd —— Tver and Yaroslavl battalions.

———— 3rd —— Vladimir and Kostroma battalions.

7th ———— 1st —— Moscow and Ryazan battalions.

———— 2nd —— Tula and Orel battalions.

———— 3rd —— Voronezh and Tambov battalions.

8th ———— 1st —— Vyatka, Perm, and Ufa battalions.

9th ———— 1st —— Nizhnii-Novgorod and Simbirsk battalions.

———— 2nd —— Saratov and Penza battalions.

———— 3rd —— Kazan Regiment.

10th ———— 1st —— Georgievsk and Tiflis battalions.

11th ———— Tobolsk and Tomsk battalions and Irkutsk Regiment.

12th ———— 1st Brigade: Vilna and Minsk battalions.

———— 2nd —— Grodno and Bialystok battalions.

———— 3rd —— Zhitomir and Kamenets-Podolskii battalions [300].

**24 July 1818**– The brigades of the 2nd Region of the Internal Guard were ordered to consist of the battalions:

1st Brigade — Smolensk and Kaluga.

2nd ———— Vitebsk and Mogilev [301].

**13 August 1818**– The Astrakhan Garrison Regiment was assigned to the 2nd Brigade of the 10th Region of the Separate Corps of the Internal Guard (302).

**17 April 1820**– The Taman Garrison Regiment was assigned to the Separate Georgia Corps (303).

**20 May 1820**– The 29th Infantry Division, consisting of the Orenburg garrisons, and the 30th—consisting of the Siberia garrisons, were renamed: the first—as the 26th, and the second—as the 27th (304).

**19 October 1820**– From the Viborg Garrison Battalion, and the Kuopio Garrison Battalion that was assigned to it, the *Viborg Garrison Regiment* was formed (305).

**22 July 1822**– The Selenginsk Garrison Regiment was used to form the Étape commands established in the Siberian provinces (306).

**5 January 1823**– In the provincial capital of Krasnoyarsk (in the newly established Yenisei Province) there was formed the *Krasnoyarsk Garrison Battalion*, on a field establishment (307).

**22 June 1825**– The Georgievsk Internal Garrison Battalion was transferred to the town of Stavropol and named the *Stavropolskii Vnutrennii Garnizonnyi batalion [Stavropol Internal Garrison Battalion]* (308).

Afterwards, in December of 1825, all Garrison regiments and battalions were according to the following distribution:

**a.) Separate Caucasus Corps:**

With the 21st Infantry Division: Derbent Battalion.

—— — 22nd ———————— Vladikavkaz Regiment, of 3 battalions.

Taman Regiment, of 2 battalions.

Kizlyar Battalion.

Mozdok ———

**b.) Separate Orenburg Corps:**

26th Infantry Division, 1st Brigade: Orenburg Regiment, of 2 battalions.

Uralsk Battalion.

Orsk ————

———————— 2nd ——— Kizilsk Battalion.

1st Orenburg Line Battalion.

2nd ———— —— ————

3rd ———— —— ————

———————— 3rd ——— Verkhne-Uralsk Battalion.

Troitsk ————

Zverinogolovsk ————

4th Orenbrug Line Battalion.

### c.) Separate Siberia Corps:

27th Infantry Division, 1st Brigade: Petrovsk Battalion.

Omsk Regiment, of 3 battalions.

Tobolsk Battalion.

———————— 2nd ——— Zhelezinka Battalion.

Semipalatinsk ————

Ust-Kamenogorsk ————

Tomsk ————

Biisk ————

———————— 3rd ——— Irkutsk Regiment, of 2 battalions.

Krasnoyarsk Battalion.

### d.) Separate Corps of the Internal Guard:

1st Region, 1st Brigade: Mitau and Riga battalions.

——— 2nd —— Reval, Arensburg, and Pskov battalions.

2nd ———— 1st —— Smolensk and Kaluga battalions.

——— 2nd—— Vitebsk and Mogilev battalions.

3rd ———— 1st —— Chernigov and Kiev battalions.

——— 2nd—— Poltava, Kharkov, and Kursk battalions.

4th ———— 1st —— Kishinev and Kherson battalions.

——— 2nd —— Yekaterinoslavl and Taurica battalions.

5th ———— 1st —— Viborg Regiment, of 2 battalions.

——— 2nd —— Archangel Regiment, of 3 battalions.

——— 3rd —— Petrozavodsk and Vologda battalions.

6th ———— 1st —— St.-Petersburg and Novgorod battalions.

——— 2nd —— Tver and Yaroslavl battalions.

——— 3rd —— Vladimir and Kostroma battalions.

7th ———— 1st —— Moscow and Ryazan battalions.

——— 2nd —— Tula and Orel battalions.

——— 3rd —— Voronezh and Tambov battalions.

8th ———— 1st —— Vyatka, Perm, and Ufa battalions.

9th ———— 1st —— Nizhnii-Novgorod and Simbirsk battalions.

——— 2nd —— Saratov and Penza battalions.

——— 3rd —— Kazan Regiment, of 2 battalions.

10th —— 1st —— Stavropol and Tiflis battalions.

—— 2nd —— Astrakhan Regiment, of 3 battalions.

12th —— 1st —— Vilna and Minsk battalions.

—— 2nd —— Grodno and Bialystok battalions.

—— 3rd —— Zhitomir and Kamenets-Podolskii battalions.

Assigned to the 11th Region were the Tobolsk and Tomsk battalions and the Irkutsk Regiment, which belonged to the Separate Siberia Corps (309).

# NOTES

(173) Highest Order.

(174) PSZ, Vol. XLIII, part II, pg. 12, No. 20,672, and pg. 14, No. 20,674, and Vol. XXVII, pg. 604, No. 20,764, and pg. 679, No. 20,804.

(175) PSZ, Vol. XXVIII, pg. 368, No. 21,331, and Vol. XLIII, part II, pg. 29, No. 21,665.

(176) PSZ, Vol. XXVIII, pg. 1,190, No. 21,887.

(177) PSZ, Vol. XXIX, pg. 696, No. 22,249, and Highest confirmed List of Artillery brigades, 23 August, 1806, and pg. 698, No. 22,252.

(178) Highest confirmed distribution of the companies of the 10th and 11th Artillery Regiments and 16th, 17th, and 18th Artillery Brigades, 11 September, 1806.

(179) PSZ, Vol. XXIX, pg. 1,011, No. 22,453, and an Historical Description of Artillery Companies, from 1806 to 1812, held in the Archive of the Inspection Department of the Ministry of War. It was at first proposed for this brigade to form six Light and two Horse companies, but this was canceled.

(180) Historical Description of Artillery Companies, referred to in the preceding note.

(181) PSZ, Vol. XXIX, pg. 1,210, No. 22,545.

(182) Historical Description of Artillery Companies, referred to in Note 179.

(183) Ibid.

(184) PSZ, Vol. XXX, pg. 1,186, No. 23,882.

(185) PSZ, Vol. XXXI, pg. 354, No. 24,352.

(186) PSZ, Vol. XXXI, pg. 531, No. 24,504.

(187) PSZ, Vol. XXXI, pg. 545, No. 24,514.

(188) Highest Order.

(189) Historical Description of Artillery Companies, referred to in Note 179.

(190) PSZ, Vol. XXXI, pg. 835 and 836, No. 24,763.

(191) Historical Description of Artillery Companies, referred to in Note 179.

(192) PSZ, Vol. XXXI, pg. 903, No. 24,783.

(193) PSZ, Vol. XXXI, pg. 848, No. 24,784.

(194) PSZ, Vol. XXXI, pg. 909, No. 24,884.

(195) PSZ, Vol. XXXII, pg. 229, No. 25,056.

(196) Historical Description of Artillery Companies, referred to in Note 179.

(197) Ibid.

(198) Ibid.

(199) Order of the Chief of HIS IMPERIAL MAJESTY'S Headquarters, from 26 July, 1816, № 24.

(200) PSZ, Vol. XXXIV, pg. 445, No. 26,963, and Vol. XXIV, pg. 780, No. 27,066.

(201) Highest confirmed List of Artillery brigades and companies, by numbers, 18 April, 1819.

(202) PSZ, Vol. XXXVII, pg. 207, No. 28,276.

(203) Highest Order and List of forces for 1820.

(204) PSZ, Vol. XXXVIII, pg. 161, No. 29,010.

(205) PSZ, Vol. XLIII, part II, pg. 20, No. 20,794.

(206) Highest Order.

(207) PSZ, Vol. XLIII, part II, pg. 40, No. 20,071.

(208) PSZ, Vol. XXXI, pg. 393, No. 24,383.

(209) PSZ, Vol. XXXI, pg. 484, No. 24,460.

(210) Highest Order.

(211) Archive of the Inspection Department of the Ministry of War, Book with List of forces for 1812.

(212) PSZ, Vol. XXXII, pg. 488, No. 25,297.

(213) PSZ, Vol. XXXIII, pg. 457, No. 26,069.

(214) PSZ, Vol. XLIII, part II, sect. I, pg. 29, No. 26,213.

(215) PSZ, Vol. XXXIV, pg. 325, No. 26,888.

(216) PSZ, Vol. XXXV, pg. 569, No. 27,537.

(217) PSZ, Vol. XXXVIII, pg. 157, No. 29,008.

(218) PSZ, Vol. XXXVIII, pg. 159, No. 29,009.

(219) PSZ, Vol. XXXVIII, pg. 161, No. 29,010.

(220) PSZ, Vol. XXXVIII, pg. 581, No. 29,155.

(221) Report of the Chief of HIS IMPERIAL MAJESTY'S Headquarters to His Imperial Highnessthe Inspector General of Engineers, 21 February, 1823, No. 344.

(222) Report of His Imperial Highness the Inspector General of Engineers to the Acting Chief of HIS IMPERIAL MAJESTY'S Headquarters, 14 August, 1823, No. 1,345.

(223) PSZ, Vol. XXXVIII, pg. 1,220, No. 29,612.

(224) List of forces for 1825.

(225) PSZ, Vol. XXXVI, pg. 165, No. 27,786.

(226) Order of the Chief of HIS IMPERIAL MAJESTY'S Headquarters, from 25 October, 1819, № 55.

(227) PSZ, Vol. XXXVII, pg. 210, No. 28,278.
(228) PSZ, Vol. XXXVII, pg. 443, No. 28,417.
(229) Report of the Chief of HIS IMPERIAL MAJESTY'S Headquarters to His Imperial Highness the Tsesarevich Constantine Pavlovich, from 1 October, 1820, № 1,753.
(230) PSZ, Vol. XXXVII, pg. 510, No. 28,468.
(231) PSZ, Vol. XXXVIII, pg. 57, No. 28,913.
(232) PSZ, Vol. XXXVII, pg. 153, No. 29,004.
(233) Highest Order.
(234) Highest Order.
(235) PSZ, Vol. XXVI, pg. 722, No. 19,951, and List of garrisons for 1801.
(236) Directive of the Government Military College, 17 August, 1801.
(237) PSZ, Vol. XXII, pg. 76, No. 20,188.
(238) Highest confirmed Personnel Tables, 30 April, 1802.
(239) Highest Order of 14 August, 1803, and Signed Order to the Military College, from 3 August, 1803.
(240) Highest Order.
(241) Highest Order.
(242) PSZ, Vol. XXVIII, pp. 3 and 4, No. No. 21,114 and 21,115.
(243) PSZ, Vol. XXVIII, pg. 240, No. 24,240.
(244) Highest Order and PSZ, Vol. XXVIII, pg. 476, No. 21,426, and pg. 715, .No. №21,533 and 21,534.
(245) Highest Order.
(246) Highest Order.
(247) PSZ, Vol. XXIX, pg. 375, No. 22,178.
(248) Highest Order.
(249) PSZ, Vol. XXIX, pg. 861, No. 22,354.
(250) PSZ, Vol. XXIX, pg. 1,188, No. 22,529.
(251) PSZ, Vol. XXIX, pg. 1,363, No. 22,731.
(252) PSZ, Vol. XXX, pg. 58, No. No. 22,807 and 22,808.
(253) Highest Order and PSZ, Vol. XXX, pg. 1,213, No. 23,908.
(254) PSZ, Vol. XXX, pg. 1,219, No. 23,921.
(255) PSZ, Vol. XXXI, pg. 25, No. 24,079.
(256) Highest Order.
(257) Highest Order.
(258) PSZ, Vol. XXXI, pg. 335, No. 24,331, § 7.
(259) Highest Order.
(260) Highest Order.
(261) Highest Order and PSZ, Vol. XXXI, pg. 537, No. 24,505.
(262) PSZ, Vol. XXXI, pp. 631 and 632, No. 24,615, and pg. 678, No. 24,675.
(263) PSZ, Vol. XXXI, pp. 587, No. 24,561.
(264) PSZ, Vol. XXXI, pp. 593, No. 24,568, and List of the Internal Guard for 1811 and 1812.
(265) Highest Order.
(266) Highest Order.
(267) Highest Order.
(268) Highest Order addressed to the Minister of War, 6 November, 1811.
(269) Highest Order.
(270) Highest Order.
(271) Highest Order.
(272) Highest Order.
(273) Highest Order.
(274) Highest Order.
(275) Highest Order.
(276) Highest Order.
(277) PSZ, Vol. XXXII, pg. 282, No. 25,081, §§ 1, 2, 3, etc.
(278) Highest Order.
(279) PSZ, Vol. XXXII, pg. 449, No. 25,256.
(280) Highest Order.
(281) Highest Order.
(282) Highest Order.
(283) PSZ, Vol. XXXII, pg. 545, No. 25,352.
(284) List of forces for 1814.
(285) PSZ, Vol. XXXII, pg. 715, No. 25,513.
(286) Report from the Vladikavkaz Regiment, for February, 1814.

(287) PSZ, Vol. XXXII, pg. 144, No. 25,863, and List of forces for 1815.
(288) PSZ, Vol. XXXIII, pg. 471, No. 26,118.
(289) Highest Order.
(290) PSZ, Vol. XXXIII, pg. 589, No. 26,616.
(291) PSZ, Vol. XXXIII, pg. 932, No. 26,350.
(292) PSZ, Vol. XL, general appendix, pg. 109, No. 26,356.
(293) PSZ, Vol. XXXIII, pg. 995, No. 26,405.
(294) PSZ, Vol. XXXIII, pg. 1,013, No. 26,426.
(295) PSZ, Vol. XXXIII, pg. 1,038, No. 26,447.
(296) Highest Order.
(297) PSZ, Vol. XXXIV, pg. 9, No. 26,599.
(298) PSZ, Vol. XXXIV, pg. 183, No. 26,777.
(299) PSZ, Vol. XXXIV, pg. 297, No. 26,855.
(300) PSZ, Vol. XXXV, pg. 122, No. 27,284.
(301) PSZ, Vol. XXXV, pg. 359, No. 27,432.
(302) PSZ, Vol. XXXV, pg. 447, No. 27,474.
(303) PSZ, Vol. XXXVII, pg. 161, No. 28,235.
(304) PSZ, Vol. XXXVII, pg. 207, No. 28,276.
(305) PSZ, Vol. XXXVII, pg. 465, No. 28,442.
(306) PSZ, Vol. XXXVIII, pg. 469, No. 29,129, § 14.
(307) PSZ, Vol. XXXVIII, pg. 699, No. 29,254.
(308) PSZ, Vol. XL, pg. 333, No. 30,391.
(309) List of battalions of the Internal Guard for 1825.

*Treaty of Tilsitz. Meeting of the two emperors in a pavilion set up on a raft in the middle of the Neman River. By. A Rohen*

# VIII - ARMY FOOT ARTILLERY (*ARMEISKAYA PESHAYA ARTILLERIYA*)

**9 April 1801-** Lower ranks of Field [*Polevaya*]—or Army Foot [*Armeiskaya Peshaya*]—Artillery were ordered to cut off their **curls** [*pukli*] and have **queues** [*kosy*] only 7 inches long [4 *vershka*], tying them midway down the collar (1).

**19 May 1801-** Train [*Furshtatskii*] officers of Foot Artillery were prescribed the same uniforms as other officers of this artillery, except that the pants were green [*shtany zelenyya*] (2).

**13 May 1801 –** Lower ranks of **Foot Artillery** were given **dark-green coats** of the same pattern as prescribed in 1802 for lower ranks of Army infantry, with collar, cuffs, and skirt turnbacks of black cloth, with red cloth piping along the edges of the collar, cuff-flaps, and turnbacks, and lined with black kersey [*karazeya*]. Pants, boots, hats, and other uniform items were issued the same as for their army infantry equivalents, except that the first were light green as before (Illus. 1603). Generals and field and company-grade officers were ordered to also have uniforms of the infantry pattern but with the same colors as for the lower ranks (Illus. 1604), while their shabracks and holsters [*chepraki i chushki*] were left dark green with one row of gold galloon (4).

**11 June 1801–** Small clothes [*nizhnee plat'e*] for all combatant ranks of the Foot Artillery, and in addition the gloves of noncommissioned and commissioned officers, were to be white instead of a light pale yellow [*svetlopalevyi*] (4).

**27 March 1802–** Combatant ranks of the Foot Artillery were ordered to have **shoulder straps** by battalions: in the 1st Battalion – red, in the 2nd – white, in the 3rd – yellow, in the 4th – light raspberry [*svetlomalinovyi*], in the 5th – turquoise [*biryuzovyi*], in the 6th – pink [*rozovyi*], in the 7th – light green, in the 8th – gray, in the 9th – lilac [*lilovyi*], in the 10th – dark blue [*sinii*], and the 11th – pale yellow [*palevyi*], in the 12th – orange, in the 13th – camel colored [*verblyuzhii*], and in Pontoon Depots – light green. Noncombatant and train lower ranks were given the same uniform as noncombatant lower ranks of the Army infantry had as this time, but with a black standing collar (without piping), black facings, and a shoulder strap on the left should only, in the battalion color (5).

**27 October 1802-** While on the march with troops or on detached duties, generals and field and company-grade officers were ordered to wear, instead of white pants [*pantalony*], gray **riding trousers** [*reituzy*], with brass buttons and leather lining, identical to those established at this time for officers of Army infantry and cavalry (6).

**16 June 1803–** Officers of the train were ordered to wear **grey small cloths** (7).

**29 June 1803-** New patterns for the *shabrack* and *holster* were designated for generals and field and company-grade officers, of dark-green cloth with two rows of gold galloon, with black cloth between these rows, and with red cloth piping along the edges (Illus. 1605) (8).

**19 August 1803–** Lower ranks were given cloth **shakos** [*shapki*] in place of the tricorn hat [*shlyapa*]. These had leather visors in the same style as introduced at this time in musketeer regiments (Illus. 1606) (9).

**17 December 1803–** A new authorization table of **weaponry and accouterments** for artillery regiments was confirmed, based on which privates, i.e. canoneers and gun handlers [*kanoniry i gandlangery*] kept the same uniforms as laid down on 13 May 1801 with subsequent changes, except that mounted gun handlers were given gray riding trousers with covered buttons and leather lining, exactly as used by the cavalry from 1801 to 1814. Artillery privates had swords [*shpagi*] (with broad blades [*tesachnye klinki*]), swordbelts, knapsacks, and water bottles all of the same patterns as for the infantry, while powder flasks [*porokhovyya natruski*] were the same as used during the preceding reign (Illus. 1606).

**Bombardiers** [*bombardiry*, i.e corporals] were distinguished from cannoneers and gun handlers only by gold lace on cuffs of the coat (Illus. 1607).

**Fireworkers** [*feierverkery*, i.e. sergeants], officer candidates [*yunkera*], and first sergeants [*fel'dfebeli*] did not carry powder flasks, but had gold galloon on the collar and cuffs of the coat, as well as along the lower edge of the shako. Following the example of noncommissioned officers in grenadier, musketeer, and jäger regiments, they were prescribed gloves, canes, and they had the same colored rings [*trinchiki*] on the sword knot and the same center to the top tuft [*kist'*] on shakos that these ranks had (Illus. 1608).

**Distinguished officer candidates** [*portupei-yunkera*] had silver sword knots of the pattern for infantry officers.

**Drummers** [*barabanshchiki*] had chevrons sewn on the coat, and drums, that were exactly the same as laid down for drummers in the Army infantry, while the drum sticks were black (Illus. 1609).

**Battalion drummers** had chevrons and drums like those for battalion drummers in the Army infantry, and the same galloon, gloves, canes, tufts on top of the shako, and sword-knot tassels that these personnel had, as authorized for noncommissioned officers (Illus 1609).

**Musicians** [*muzykanty*] (two each for the bassoon, French horn, clarinet, flute, and trumpet), at first authorized only for the 1st Artillery Regiment, were uniformed identically to battalion drummers (10).

**Officers**, including generals, were left with the uniforms set forth for them on 13 May and 11 June 1801, except that it was directed that they were to wear hats with a tall plume and a button loop of narrow gold galloon (Illus. 1610) (11).

**Officers of the train** differed from combatant officers only in that they had gray small clothes (Illus. 1611) (12).

**Noncombatant lower ranks**, including those of the train, kept the uniforms prescribed for them on 27 March 1802, with only the hat being replaced by the shako instituted on 19 August 1803. This shako did not have two pompons as for combatants, but only a single lower tuft. Of these ranks all those having noncommissioned officer status—nurses [*nadzirateli bol'nykh*], doctors' assistants [*fel'dshera*], clerks [*pisarya*], and supply train noncommissioned officers—had, just as did combatant noncommissioned officers, galloon, gloves, canes, shako pompons, and sword knots. In addition, for riding horses train noncommissioned officers were issued gray riding trousers with leather (Illus. 1612). Barbers [*tsiryul'niki*], who were prescribed a sword [*shpaga*] (without a sword knot), sword belt, and pouch for shaving instruments and other items, did not wear galloon lace, and had pompons on the shako in the same colors as did privates (Illus. 1613). Lazarette orderlies [*lazaretnye sluzhiteli*], master craftsmen ]*masterovye*] and their apprentices, farriers [*konovaly*], and train personnel [*furleity*] were uniformed the same as barbers except they did not have the latters' pouch, nor were they authorized a sword (Illus. 1614). All these ranks, except for train personnel, had knapsacks and water flasks. Instead of knapsacks, train personnel were issued valises [*chemodany*] of gray cloth (13).

**Doctors** [*lekarya*] and **auditors** [*auditory*, i.e. legal assistants] were uniformed completely the same as doctors and auditors in all the other branches of the Army (14).

Regiments were distinguished from one another by their **shoulder straps** and the center of the privates' **shako pompon**, which were prescribed to be the following colors:

1st Artillery Regiment – red.
2nd — — — — white.
3rd — — — — yellow.
4th — — — — light raspberry.
5th — — — — turquoise.     6th — — — — pink.     7th — — — — light green.
8th — — — — dark blue.
9th — — — — orange.
Pontoon — — — black.

In the first battalions of all these regiments the lower and upper pompons on the shako were white, and in second battalions – red. The middle of the pompon was, for privates, the same color as the shoulder strap, while for noncommissioned officers it was black and orange. Pompons on train shakos were in two colors: dark green and that prescribed for the shoulder strap. For privates' sword knots the acorn [*derevyashka*] was the same color as the shoulder strap while loops [*gaechki*] and rings [*trinchiki*] varied by company: in first Battery companies – white, in second Light companies – sky blue, in third Light companies – orange, and in fourth Battery companies – red. For noncommissioned officers sword knot rings were white, black, and orange (15).

Each company of Foot Field Artillery was issued **entrenching tools** [*shantsevyi instrument*]: 20 axes and 20 iron shovels, with cases, as for Army Infantry regiments.

In a Battery company the **guns** were four half-pood unicorns [*polupudovye yedinorogy*, a half pood, or pud, being eighteen pounds] and two 3-pounder unicorns; in a Light company – four 12-pounder unicorns and eight 6-pounder cannons (18).

**5 March 1805** – The round powder flasks used by bombardiers, cannoneers, and gun handlers were replaced by **pouches** [*lyadunki*] of black leather with a round brass plate of a pattern and size similar to the plates on cavalry pouches at this time (Illus. 1615). The crossbelt for this pouch was prescribed to be 2 1/2 inches [*2/1/2 dyuima*] wide, while fittings to the crossbelt were according the following list:

Prickers [*protravniki*] (one iron and the other brass), 7/8 inch [*1/2 vershka*] long to the bend in the ring [*do zagiba kol'tsa*], the bend being 1/2 inch [*1/3 vershka*].

Chain (brass) to the prickers: for tall men – 8 3/4 inches [*5 vershkov*], men of middle height – 8 inches [*4 1/2 vershka*], and short men – 7 inches [*4 vershka*].

The first sewn-on attachment on the crossbelt, to which the chain fastened, was 1 3/4 inches [*1 vershok*] below the shoulder strap.

The second attachment, through which passed the prickers, was sewn on 8 inches from the first for tall men, 7 inches for men of middle height, and 6 1/2 inches [3 3/4 vershka] for short men.

The third tab, into which the ends of the prickers were placed, was positioned 7 1/2 inches [4 1/4 vershka] below the second.

The sizes of the tabs were: first or uppermost – 2 1/2 inches long, 3/4 inches wide; second or middle – 3 1/2 inches long, 3/4 inches wide; and third or lowest – 4 inches long, 2 inches wide.

The first two tabs were rectangular, but for the third the lower end was rounded (17).

**16 March 1805**– HIGHESTconfirmation was given to a table of uniform clothing, accouterments, and weaponry for the **Pontoon Regiment** formed from the Pontoon Depot. Based on this table, privates or pontoniers [*pontonery*] of the 3rd and 2nd, i.e. junior, classes received the exact same uniforms and weapons as gun handlers and cannoneers of Artillery regiments, with the only exceptions being that the shoulder straps and center of the shako pompon were to be black, and pants were to be gray. Along with this, mounted personnel were prescribed riding trousers (Illus. 1615). 1st Class Pontoniers [*Pontonery 1-i stat'i*] were distinguished, similarly to artillery bombardiers, by gold galloon on the cuffs (Illus 1616).

All other ranks—fireworkers, officer candidates, distinguished officer candidates, first sergeants, drummers, officers, and all noncombatants holding the same titles as in Artillery regiments—were uniformed and armed in accordance with the regulations in force for those regiments, with only the aforementioned difference in colors for the shoulder straps, shako pompons, and small clothes (Illus. 1616 and 1617) (18).

**23 December 1805**– In order to avoid certain negative aspects encountered during battles with the enemy, Artillery generals and field and company-grade officers with the forces of the **Caucasus Inspectorate** were ordered to wear **shakos** in all respects similar to those of the soldiers, except instead of worsted pompons they were to have silver ones with a mixture of black and orange silk (Illus. 1618). These shakos were stipulated to be only for campaign use and during military operations, and hats were to be worn the rest of the time (19).

**27 January 1806**– The newly formed **10th and 11th Artillery Regiments** were assigned shoulder straps: pale yellow for the first, and black for the second (20).

**1 July 1806**– There were the same changes in uniforms of **doctors** in the Foot Artillery as were described in detail above for Army infantry and cavalry (21).

**1 October 1806** – The **sheepskin warm coats** [*ovchinnyya fufaiki*] authorized for lower ranks up to now were withdrawn (22).

**2 December 1806**– Lower ranks were ordered to cut their **hair** short; generals, though, and field and company-grade officers, were in this regard allowed to proceed according to their personal wishes (22).

In this same year HIGHESTconfirmation was given to regulations drawn up under the direct supervision of General Graf Arakcheev, Inspector of all Artillery at that time, regarding the cut, tailoring, colors, fit, and use of **uniform items** and**accouterments** for the lower ranks. These were partly in accord with the regulations established on 15 January 1802 for personnel of the Army infantry, with the above tables of 17 December 1803 and 16 March 1805, and partly with some changes and additions that included the following:

a) When combatant lower ranks were ordered to have the greatcoat carried with them, then it was to be fastened to the knapsak strap after having been tightly rolled into a tube 14 inches [8 vershkov] long (Illus 1619).

b) A greatcoat, rolled up in this way and tied at the two ends with special 1-inch wide whitened straps, was to be fastened by these straps to the knapsack strap by a loop sewn on top of the knapsack (Illus. 1619).

c) The knapsack with or without the flask and rolled greatcoat attached was to be worn over the man's right shoulder, close to the shoulders and a little higher to the right, diagonally so that during any movement the arms were free to move (Illus 1619).

d) When knapsacks were without greatcoats, the knapsack strap was to be shortened, being tightened so that the knapsack was right at the shoulders (Illus. 1620).     e) Mounted cannoneers with the guns and caissons were not to wear knapsacks with greatcoats and flasks, but rather pack these behind the horse's saddle, placing the knapsack with all its internal contents and the rolled up greatcoat held to it on the cushion [*podushka*], and then attaching all this behind the saddle by three whitened straps located there, with iron buckles (Illus. 1621). From the right side of the knapsack there were to be hung a rope for general use and forage [*arkannaya i furazhnaya verevka*], 1/2 inch thick and 30 feet [5 sazhen] long and coiled into a ring the same size as the circumference of the knapsack, with the ends tied to the knapsack's middle buckle under the cover flap. The water flask was to be attached over this coil of rope, its straps being held by the first separate strap that fastened the greatcoat and knapsack (Illus. 1622).

f) When personnel were detached to accompany horses for cut forage, then each company's detailed fireworkers and bombardirs were to wear full accouterments but without the pouch, on saddled horses with knapsacks with greatcoats and flasks behind the saddle (Illus. 1623). Gun handlers, for whom saddlers were not authorized, were to leave their knapsacks and flasks with their section baggage [artel'naya povozka], while the greatcoat was to be over the right shoulder, rolled along its whole length and tied at the ends with whitened straps (Illus 1623).     g) All noncombatant ranks, including junior train-masters [unter-furmeistery] and train personnel, were to wear knapsacks with rolled greatcoats and water flasks over the right shoulder, exactly as related for combatants (Illus. 1624 and 1625). h) Junior train-masters and train personnel who had valises instead of knapsacks were to pack these, along with their greatcoats and flasks, behind the saddles of their horses. If the train personnel were not mounted and instead leading pack animals, then all these thing were to be left with the wagons (24).

**10 March 1807**– **Canes** were withdrawn for officers and noncommissioned officers (25).

**22 September 1807**– With the reorganization of Army Foot Artillery from regiments to brigades, these latter were ordered to have **shoulder straps** of the following colors:

In the 2nd Brigade (the Guard Artillery formed the 1st Brigade) – white, in the 3rd – white with red piping, in the 4th – yellow, in the 5th – yellow with red piping, in the 6th – black, in the 7th – light raspberry, in the 8th, light raspberry with black piping, in the 9th – turquoise, in the 10th turquoise with red piping, in the 11th – pink, in the 12th – pink with dark green piping, in the 13th – dark blue, in the 14th – red with black piping, in the 15th – white with black piping, in the 16th – dark green, in the 17th – dark green with red piping, in the 18th – dark blue with red piping, in the 19th orange, in the 20th – orange with black piping, in the 21st – red, in the 22nd – black with red piping, in the 23rd (Siberia) – lilac, in the Reserve St.-Petersburg Brigade – gray, in the Reserve Kiev Brigade – gray with red piping, and in the Reserve Moscow Brigade – lilac with red piping (26).

**23 September 1807**– All companies in a brigade were ordered to have **sword-knot** acorns of the same color as the shoulder straps, while loops and rings were to be white in the first Battery company, red in the second, sky blue in the first Light, green in the second, and black in the Pontoon company (27). As for the [shako's – M.C.] small pompons [kistochki or repeiki] and tufts [sultanchiki or kardonchiki], the outside was to be white as previously while the center was the same color as the shoulder strap, ignoring any piping this may have around it (28).

**23 December 1807**– Lower ranks were given new pattern summer and winter **pants** of the pattern confirmed at this same time for Grenadier and Musketeer regiments, i.e. with spats for the first, and for the second—leather trim or leggings [kragi], with seven brass buttons (29).

**3 January 1808** – Lower ranks throughout the Army Foot Artillery were ordered to have just **red shoulder straps**, with the brigade number of yellow worsted cord sewn on, 1-3/4 inches [1 vershok] long, and when there was no number, then with the initial letters of the title, namely: in the Siberia Brigade – the letter C., in the St.-Petersburg Reserve Brigade – C. .P., in the Kiev Reserve Brigade – K.P., and in the Moscow Reserve Brigade – M.P. (30). Field and company-grade officers were given **epaulettes** with a red cloth field and the brigade number embroidered in gold, similar to the description for Army regiments but without a twisted cord around it, and with a thick tongue [nakladka] (Illus 1626 and 1627). Generals were directed to have epaulettes without numbers (31). Along with this there was a new allocation of colors for **sword knots** and the **pompons and tassels** of shakos and forage caps:

In the first Battery companies of all brigades – the ring and loop of the sword knot and the loop above the tassel on forage caps were to be white.

In second Battery companies – red.

In first Light companies – sky blue.

In second Light companies – green.

In Pontoon companies – black.

In all these companies sword-knot acorns were to be red; pompons [kisti ili repeiki] and tufts [sultanchiki] of shakos, and the tassels [kisti] on forage caps – white with a red center.

For noncommissioned officers – sword-knot rings and shako tufts remained of of three colors as before: white, black, and orange (32).

**7 March 1808**– For the entire Foot Artillery **sword belts** [portupei] were ordered to be worn not around the waist but over the right shoulder, as described for Grenadier and Musketeer regiments, but without the frog for the bayonet scabbard, which was not authorized for artillerymen (33). From this same time the cloth **shakos** introduced in 1803 began to be lined with black leather to make them stronger, and the visors for them were sewn on. After this they received the name *kiver* (Illus. 1628) (34).

**8 March 1808** – For the successful bombardment of the Svartholm fortress, field and company-grade officers of Colonel Belgard's Battery Company of the 21st Artillery Brigade were ordered to have as a badge of distinction gold **embroidered button loops** [*petlitsy*]: two on each side of the collar and three on each cuff flap (Illus. 1629) (35).

**14 July 1808** – For lower ranks of the Foot Artillery the round **knapsacks** were exchanged for rectangular ones of the same pattern as those established at this time for Grenadier and Musketeer regiments. Along with it was set forth as a rule for these personnel to carry the greatcoat, when it was not being worn, in accordance with the rules set forth above for Grenadiers (Illus. 1630) coat (36).

**14 September 1808**– Lower ranks of the Foot Artillery were ordered to have **gray cloth pants** instead of white ones (37).

**8 October 1808**– Instead of a ribbon [*bant*], the **shako** of Foot Artillery lower ranks was to have a **plate** [*gerb*] of two crossed brass cannons with a similarly brass bomb [*bombochka*] (Illus. 1630) (38).

**2 November 1808**- The **pants** authorized on 23 December 1807, with leggings [*kragi*] in the winter and spats in the summer, were kept only for combatant lower ranks, while for noncombatants the pants as well as the boots were directed to be of the patterns established on 17 December 1803 (39).

**5 November 1808**- Company-grade officers of the Foot Artillery, when the troops were wearing **knapsacks**, were ordered to also have them, of the same pattern in all respects as was established for lower ranks (40).

**12 November 1808**- When not on duty, field and company-grade officers were allowed to wear dark-green cloth **pants** instead of white ones (41).

**11 February 1809**– All **noncombatant lower ranks** not holding noncommissioned officer status were given a new pattern **cap** [*shapka*] in place of the shako [*kiver*] and forage cap with tassel, identical to those which were introduced at this time in Army Infantry regiments, but with a black band and red piping around its edges (Illus 1631) (42).

**4 April 1809**- **Noncommissioned officers** were ordered to have **galloon** not on the lower and side edges of the collar, but on the upper and side edges (Illus. 1632) (43).

**20 April 1809** – The change in the manner of wearing the **knapsack**, introduced at this time for Army Infantry, i.e. with the addition of a third strap running crossways, was extended to Artillery and Pontoon companies (Illus. 1632) (44).

**24 May 1809**– Field and company-grade officers of the Foot Artillery, including Pontoon officers, were given **gorgets** [*znaki*] of the same pattern as those established in 1808 for grenadier and musketeer officers (45).

**8 June 1809**–The plumage on **generals' hats** was discontinued and the former pattern of buttonhole was replaced with a new one made of four thick, twisted cords, of which the two middle ones were intertwined with each other as if in a plait (46).

**11 June 1809**– Cords [*etishkety*] were given to the **shakos** of lower ranks: red for privates and multicolored white, black, and orange for noncommissioned officers and musicians (Illus. 1633)(47). Along with this pompons for all privates were ordered to be red, while for noncommissioned officers they were as before, two quarters white and two quarters black with orange (Illus. 1633)(48).

**28 August 1809**– In order to distinguish officers' coats of the Foot Field Artillery from those of Jäger regiments, generals and field and company-grade officers of the Artillery were ordered to have **red cloth piping** not only along the top and sides of the collar, but also along the lower edge (Illus. 1634)(49).

**8 October 1809**– Lower ranks of Battery, Light, and Pontoon companies were ordered to have **dark-green winter pants**, the same color as the coat, and mounted gun handlers and train noncommissioned officers were additionally to have black leather along the inner seam. After this, gray riding trousers were no longer authorized for them (Illus 1634) (50).

**6 December 1809**– Field and company-grade officers of the Foot Field Artillery were ordered to wear a **shako** [*kiver*] instead of the hat when in formation, of the same pattern as established at this time for field and company-grade officers of Fusilier (in Grenadier regiments) and Musketeer battalions, only with the same plate as artillery privates (Illus. 1634) (51), but when not in formation the hat was kept as before, except with a shortened plume (Illus. 1634)(52).

In this same year the **powdering of the hair** was completely discontinued for officers, and it was permitted for them when off duty to wear **frock coats** [*sertuki*] like the officers' frock coats in the Army infantry, except with black collar and cuffs piped red, and black lining (Illus. 1635) (53).

**24 September 1810**- **Knapsack straps** were ordered to be stitched on the edges, in the manner of crossbelts and swordbelts, and have a bend at each shoulder so that they do not wear away the coat and constrict a man under his arms (54).

**17 January 1811**– Instead of the multicolored **cords** on their **shakos**, noncommissioned officers and musicians of the Foot Field Artillery were to have red ones, the tassels being white with black and orange mixed in (Illus. 1636) (55).

**25 October 1811**– Lower ranks of the Foot Field Artillery were given dark-green **caps** [*shapki*] of a new pattern, with a black band that had the brigade number in red cord sewn on in front. The pattern of these caps was exactly like that for the forage caps introduced on 23 September of this year in Grenadier and other Army infantry regiments, and by which the companies in each branch were distinguished by piping, in this case of the following colors:

    In Battery companies – black on top around the cap; red around both edges of the band (Illus. 1637)(56).

    In Light companies – black on top around the cap; red around the top edge of the band (Illus. 1637)(57).

    In Pontoon companies – red on top around the cap (Illus. 1637)(58).

**3 November 1811**- **Gloves** were abolished for noncommissioned officers, and to replace them in cold weather they were allowed to wear cloth mittens [*rukavitsy*] sewn from old dress coats (59).

**17 December 1811**- **Noncombatant lower ranks** of the Foot Artillery, in place of the uniforms they had since 1802, were given new ones identical to those established at this time for noncombatant lower ranks in Grenadier and Musketeer regiments, but with black piping and the brigade number in red cord on the cap (Illus. 1638)(60).

**10 February 1812**- Noncombatant lower ranks were ordered to have **shoulder straps** on their caftan coats [*kaftany*] and greatcoats of the same color and pattern as the shoulder straps of combatant ranks (61), and about this time there were the following changes in the uniforms of combatant ranks of the Foot Artillery:

    1) New-pattern **shakos** were issued, lower than before, with a big indentation or widening upwards, and sloping upwards at the sides. They lacked the sewn-on neck flaps or ear flaps, which from this time on were worn separately (Illus. 1639).

    2) The high **collars** which opened diagonally upwards were replaced by lower ones closed with small hooks (Illus. 1639).

    3) Lower combatant ranks were given **gaiters** and officers **high boots** reaching up to the knees, the first having nine buttons (Illus. 1639).

    4) Instead of the brigade number, it was ordered that **shoulder straps** and epaulettes were to have the company number and the initial letter of its title, for example: in the 5th Battery Company – 5 followed by a Cyrillic B; in the 17th Light Company – 17 followed by a Cyrillic L; in the 1st Pontoon Company – 1 followed by a Cyrillic P, and so on (Illus. 1639).

    5) In order to lessen their expenditures, officers were allowed to have **white shako cords and sword knots** instead of silver ones, and stamped brass fittings to the epaulettes instead of gold (62).

**13 April 1813**– In the Foot Artillery, Battery Companies No. 14, 23, and 24, and Light Companies No. 33 and 47 were granted **badges** [*znaki*] for the shako, with the inscription "For Distinction" ["*Za otlichie*"], following the style for Army infantry regiments, i.e. in the form of a shield, and which was accepted as standard for all Foot Artillery companies which would receive this award in the subsequent years of Emperor Alexander I's reign (Illus. 1640) (63). Apart from these badges, officers of the indicated companies were granted **gold button loops**: two on each side of the coat collar and three on each cuff flap. This was subsequently extended to all other companies that received the badge for distinction (Illus. 1640)(64). (Note: a detailed listing of Artillery companies and other units which received shako badges will be found later, in the separate chapter "Badges for Distinction.")

**20 May 1814**– The **gray riding trousers** with buttons and leather lining prescribed since 1802 for field and company-grade officers of Foot Artillery were replaced by similarly gray ones with black **double stripes** [*lampasy*] with red piping (both stripes and piping being of cloth), and without leather lining (Illus. 1641) (65).

**In 1814**, it was ordered that the **cockades** on officers' hats have white tape around them, later replaced by silver, and in 1815 Artillery **drum majors** were directed to be uniformed according to the patterns for Army drum majors, with the only difference being the appropriate changes in coat colors (Illus. 1642). The placement of **chevrons** sewn on musicians' and drummers' coats was also changed, these coats being single-breasted with small hooks instead of buttons, and with tape or lace [*tes'ma ili bason*] on both sides of the opening, following the example, as stated above, of musicians and drummers of Army infantry (Illus. 1642) (66).

**24 January 1816**– **Scabbards** for short swords [*tesaki*] and officers' swords [*shpagi*] were ordered to be black throughout the Foot Field Artillery, the first being polished, and the second lacquered (67).

**10 February 1816**– Combatant lower ranks of the Foot Artillery in the Guards Corps were ordered to have **chinstraps** with smooth brass scales (Illus 1643). Other companies, as before, were not authorized these (68).

**13 April 1816** - Field and company-grade officers of the Foot Field Artillery were ordered to wear cloth **pants** with high boots only during reviews and parades, and during the rest of the time to have the riding trousers with stripes prescribed in 1814, with the exception of officers in the capitals, where they were prescribed to be in dark-green pants and high boots (69).

**16 June 1816**– Foot Artillery companies in the Grenadier Corps and the Georgia Grenadier Brigade were given **plumes** [*sultany*] for the shako, of the pattern for grenadier plumes in the Army infantry (Illus. 1643 (70).

**28 July 1816**– It was ordered that in the Foot Artillery, officers on their **epaulettes**, and lower ranks on their **shoulder straps**, have the brigade number and not that of the company, as it was until 1812 (71).

**16 November 1816**– The order of 28 August 1809 for officers in the Foot Artillery to have **red piping** all around the collar was extended to lower ranks (Illus 1643) (72).

**8 August 1817**- The size of the **forage cap** was fixed as established at this time for forage caps in Army infantry regiments (73).

**26 September 1817** – The description confirmed on this day of **shakosand accouterments**and the rules for wearing them were adopted in the Foot Artillery (Illus. 1644)(74).

**8 December 1817**- The leather **leggings** [*kragi*] on the cloth pants were ordered to have **integral spats** [*kozyrki*] of a pattern similar to the gaiter spats [*shtibletnye kozyrki*] of summer pants (Illus. 1644)(74).

**17 February 1818**– It was reaffirmed that all ranks in the Foot Artillery have **red piping** around the collar (76).

**26 June 1818**– In the Foot Artillery of the **Separate Lithuania Corps**, i.e. in the 27th and 28th Brigades (Note: on 20 May 1820 the 27th Brigade was renumbered as the 24th, and the 28th became the 25th) it was ordered to have coats with black lapels [*latskany*] (of cloth for lower ranks and velvet for officers) with red piping around their edges, and shakos with round pompons the same color as the cords. Instead of leather leggings they were to wear cloth gaiters with spats [*shtiblety s kozyrkami*], following the example of Grenadier, Infantry, and Jäger regiments in this corps (Illus. 1645 and 1646) (77).

**23 August 1818**- Combatant lower ranks of the Foot Artillery were ordered to have **shoulder straps** on coats and greatcoats that were as long as the shoulder and 2 1/8 inches wide, of the previous red color, with the brigade number 1 3/4 inches in size, cut out 7/8 inch from the lower edge of shoulder strap and backed with yellow cloth stiched around the edges of the cutout. The flaps or **wings** [*klapany ili kryltsa*] on musicians' and drummers' coats were prescribed to be of black cloth with red piping, while the tape for sewn-on trim, 7/8 inch wide, was white with a red stripe down the center for Artillery in the Grenadier Corps and the Georgia Grenadier Brigade, and in the rest of the Artillery—all white (Illus. 1647) (78).

**25 January 1819**- **Drumsticks** and **entrenching tool handles** were directed to be black throughout the Foot Artillery (79).

**16 February 1819**– Lower ranks of the Foot Artillery, when on campaign or in camps, were ordered to have **black linen covers** for the shako, plume, pouch, and coat with leggings, of the same patterns and following the same guidelines as established on 13 May 1817 for Grenadier and other regiments of Army infantry, with only the addition of letters designating the company. For example, in a first Battery company [*1 Batareinaya rota*] – 1 followed by a Cyrillic B. and R., and so on (80).

**4 April 1819**- The **spats** on the leggings were abolished (81).

**18 April 1819**– In the newly formed **Georgia Grenadier Artillery Brigade**, epaulettes and shoulder straps were ordered to have the Cyrillic letters G.B., i.e. Georgia Brigade (82).

**11 November 1819**– The following colors were assigned for **sword knots**:

In the first Battery companies of the 1st, 2nd, and 3rd Grenadier Brigades – red (Illus. 1648, a).

In the second Battery companies of these three brigades – red loop [*okolysh*], white rings and acorns (Illus. 1648, b).

In Light companies of these brigades – red loop, light blue [*svetlosinii*] rings and acorn (Illus. 1648, c).

In Park companies of these brigades – red loop, green rings and acorn (Illus. 1648, d.)

In Reserve companies of these brigades – red loop, yellow rings and acorn (Illus. 1648 e.)

In the first Battery companies of the Georgia Grenadier Brigade and all Field brigades – completely red (Illus. 1648, f).

In the second Light companies of these brigades – white (Illus. 1648, g).

In the third Light companies of these brigades – light blue (Illus. 1648, h).

In Park companies of these brigades – green (Illus. 1648, i).

In Reserve companies of these brigades – yellow (Illus. 1648, k).

In Pontoon companies (Note: on 20 April 1822 these companies were transferred to the control of the Engineers) – black (Illus. 1648, l) (83).

**9 May 1820**– It was ordered that **shakos** of the 1st, 2nd, and 3rd Grenadier Brigades and the Georgia (from 21 October 1821 – Caucasus) Grenadier Brigade have plates of the pattern for grenadiers, with two crossed cannons below (Illus. 1649 and 1650) (84).

**3 June 1820**– In the 1st, 2nd, and 3rd Grenadier Artillery Brigades it was ordered that the Cyrillic letter G be added to brigade number on **epaulettes** and **shoulder straps** (85).

**12 October 1820**- Field and company-grade officers of the Foot Artillery were given a new pattern of *gorget* [*znak*], flatter and narrower than before, without a ribbon, of the same shape and with the same rank distinctions as were established in this year for field and company-grade officers of Grenadier, Infantry, and Jäger regiments (86).

In this same year of 1820 there were changes in **musicians' and drummers' coats** which consisted of the tape on the sleeves beginning to be sewn on almost touching each other, and on the wings it was already not straight down to the lower edge, as before, but slanted; it also began to be sewn around all four edges of the collar (Illus. 1651) (87).

**21 October 1820**– It was ordered that **epaulettes** and **shoulder straps** in the Caucasus Artillery Brigade have the Cyrillic letters K.B. (88).

**27 January 1822**– Officers of the Foot Artillery were ordered to have **epaulettes** of the same pattern as for all officers of the Army infantry (89).

**26 November 1823**– In the Foot Artillery all **musicians**, even though they might not hold noncommissioned officer ranks, were ordered to have coats with gold galloon and noncommissioned officers' pompons on the shako. However, this was not extended to drummers who did not hold noncommissioned officer rank (90).

**16 January 1824** - The following changes were ordered to be carried out in the uniforms and accouterments of combatant lower ranks:

1.) **Coattails**, which up to this time had one covering the other, were to be cut so that their inner edges came together, and sewn together so they touched (Illus. 1652).

2.) The decorative end [*trinchik*] of the **shako cords**, which was to be level with the right shoulder, was to have another special loop of red cord attached to the button on the right shoulder strap, so that the shako cords stayed in place when the soldier moved about (Illus. 1652).     3.) The **cartridge pouch** was to be worn so that when the soldier bent his elbow, the distance between it and the line of the top edge of the pouch was equal to 5 1/4 inches [*3 vershka*].     4.) **Knapsack chest straps** were to be fitted so that they were between the fourth and fifth buttons of the coat, as counted from the collar (Illus. 1652) (91).

**29 March 1825**- For combatant lower ranks, for faultless service, there were established **stripes** [*nashivki*] to be sewn on the left sleeve: for 10 years service - one, for 15 years - two, for 20 years - three; one over the other, all of yellow tape (92).

# IX - ARMY HORSE ARTILLERY (*ARMEISKAYA KONNAYA ARTILLERIYA*)

**9 April 1801**- Lower ranks of Field [*Polevaya*]—or Army Horse [*Armeiskaya Konnaya*]—Artillery were ordered to cut off their **curls** [*pukli*] and have **queues** [*kosy*] only 7 inches long [*4 vershka*], tying them midway down the collar (93).

**19 May 1801**– **Train** [*Furshtatskii*] **officers** of Horse Artillery were prescribed the same uniforms as other officers of this artillery, except that the pants were green [*shtany zelenyya*] (94).

**13 May 1801** – All combatant lower ranks of Horse Artillery were ordered to have the same uniform clothing and established at this same timve for the Foot Artillery, but with the addition of **aiguilettes** [*aksel'banty*]: of yellow worsted [*garus*] for lower ranks, and gold for officers and generals (Illus. 1653) (95).

**29 May 1801**– Horse-Artillery officers as well as generals were given white **plumes** for their hats, of the pattern for their cavalry counterparts (Illus. 1653) (96).

**11 June 1801**– **Small clothes** [*nizhnee plat'e*] for all combatant ranks of the Horse Artillery, and in addition the **gloves** of noncommissioned and commissioned officers, were to be white instead of a light pale yellow [*svetlopalevyi*] (97).

**27 March 1802**– Personnel of the Horse Artillery were prescribed **new uniforms** cut like those confirmed for Dragoon regiments in this same year of 1802, in the following colors: dark-green coat with black collar, slit cuffs, and lining on the skirts and turnbacks, trimmed with red cloth, with black lining, and with an orange strap on the left shoulder. White pants, of cloth. Yellow buttons (Illus. 1654). Noncombatant and train lower ranks were given the same uniform as these personnel had in the Foot Artillery (98).

**27 October 1802**- While on the march with troops or on detached duties, generals and field and company-grade officers were ordered to wear, instead of white pants, **gray riding trousers**, with brass buttons and leather lining, identical to those established at this time for officers of Army Infantry Cavalry, and Foot Artillery (99).

**16 June 1803**– **Train officers** in the Horse Artillery were ordered to wear **grey small cloths** (100).

**22 June 1803–** In the newly formed 2nd Horse-Artillery Battalion **shoulder straps** were prescribed to be white, and in the 1st Battalion—red instead of the previous orange (101).

**18 October 1803–** All combatant lower ranks in the Horse Artillery were ordered to wear **helmets** [*kaski*] when in formation), of the pattern introduced at this time in Cuirassier and Dragoon regiments, while hats were kept for off duty (102).

**17 December 1803–** A new authorization table of **uniforms, weaponry,** and **accouterments** for Horse-Artillery battalions was confirmed, based on which lower ranks kept the same uniforms as laid down on 27 March 1802 and 18 October 1803, but without aiguilettes. New broadswords [*palashi*] were issued, with brass hilts, 29 3/4 inches [*1 arshin 1 vershok*] from the joining of the hilt to the tip of the blade, with blackened leather scabbards with a brass end piece (Illus. 1655). Sword knots (white tassels in the 1st Company, sky blue in the 2nd, yellow in the 3rd, black in the 4th, and green in the 5th), sword belts, pouches, pouch belts, water flasks (wooden, wrapped in black leather), saddles (without saddle buckets [*bushmaty*]), shabracks (dark green with pale yellow trim, monogram, and crown), and all other horse equipment, were of the patterns for dragoons (Illus. 1655 and 1656). Pistols, also identical to those for dragoons, were authorized at one per man only for those cannoneers who were not employed with the guns or ammunition caissons.

Bombardiers, as in the Foot Artillery, had gold galloon on the coat's cuffs (Illus. 1657).

Fireworkers, officer candidates, and first sergeants had coats with gold galloon on the collar and cuffs. The front of the helmet crest [*plyumazh*] was white with a light-orange stripe. The sword-knot tassel was white with black and orange. A cane and two pistols were prescribed (Illus. 1658).

Distinguished officer candidates [*portupei-yunkera*] were distinguished from the preceding noncommissioned officers only by officer-pattern cavalry sword knots on their broadswords.

Trumpeters had white chevrons on the coat and brass trumpets with red cords and tassels exactly like those prescribed for trumpets in Dragoon regiments. The helmet crest was red (Illus. 1659).

Staff-trumpeters had chevrons and trumpets (with cords and tassels colored white, black, and orange) also the same as those used by staff-trumpeters in Dragoon regiments. They also had the latter's appointments as noncommissioned officers: galloon, cane, sword knot, and top to the helmet crest (Illus. 1659) (103).

Officers, including generals, kept the uniforms they had received on 27 March 1802 and 18 October 1803. In formation, when wearing sashes, they wore the helmets established on 18 October 1803, with a hair creast (white towards the top, black towards the bottom, with an orange strip in between) (Illus. 1660), and during other times—hats with a white plume and a gold button loop of narrow galloon. Shabracks were laid down to be dark green with gold galloon, monogram, and crown (Illus. 1660) (104).

Company-grade officers of the train differed from combatant officers only in that their small clothes were gray (105).

Noncombatant lower ranks, including train personnel, were uniformed after the example of noncombatants of the Foot Artillery, with the only difference being that instead of knapsacks they had gray cloth valises, and train noncommissioned officers had spurs on their boots (106).

Auditors were not authorized for Horse-Artillery battalions, but doctors were clothed in the standard uniform prescribed for this position, as described in detail above for Grenadier regiments (107).

Fifteen axes were issued to each Horse-Artillery company, and the same number of iron shovels. Guns consisted of six 12-pounder unicorns and six 6-pounder cannons (108).

**1 July 1806–** There was the change in doctors' uniforms for the Horse Artillery as described above for Army Infantry, Cavalry, and Foot Artillery (109).

**1 October 1806 –** The **sheepskin warm coats** [*ovchinnyya fufaiki*] authorized for lower ranks up to now were withdrawn (110).

**2 December 1806–** These same ranks were ordered to cut their **hair** short; generals, though, and field and company-grade officers, were in this regard allowed to proceed according to their personal wishes (111).

In this same year the Horse Artillery was ordered to have white **forage caps** with red bands and insertions [*proshivki*], and with a tassel of both these colors (Illus. 1661). There were also established rules regarding the cut, tailoring, colors, fit, and use of **uniform items** and **accouterments**. These rules were partly in accord with the regulations established on 17 March 1802 for Dragoon regiments and the above table of 17 December 1803, and partly new, which consisted of the following:

a) "When mounted cannoneers with the guns and caissons are ordered to have the greatcoat carried with them, then it was to be placed on the valise, having been tightly rolled into a tube 16 inches [*9 vershkov*] long, i.e. the same length as the valise, and tied in two places at the ends with a white strap 1 inch wide." (Illus 1662).

b) "The valise with everything stowed inside and the greatcoat placed on top of it is to be packed behind the saddle with three whitened straps with iron buckles. From the left side of the valise there was to be hung a rope for general use and forage [*arkannaya i furazhnaya verevka*], 1/2 inch thick and 30 feet [*5 sazhen*] long and coiled into a ring the same size as the circumference of the valise, with the ends alongside that item tied to the second strap holding the valise and greatcoat. The water flask is to be attached over this coil of rope, its straps being held by the same second strap." (Illus. 1662).

c) "In this same exact manner fireworkers and mounted privates with the guns are to pack their valise, water flask, and rope for general use and forage behind the saddle, while on top of the valise goes the forage sack with or without forage. The greatcoat, though, rolled into a tube 35 inches [*1 1/4 arshina*] long, is to be laid across the horse's neck and at its midpoint tied tightly to the saddle arch, and its ends tied to the ends of the holsters so that the greatcoat is covered by the shabrack." (Illus. 1663.)

d) "When personnel are detached to accompany horses for cut forage, then each company's detailed fireworkers and privates acting as corporals [*ryadovye za yefreitorov*] are to wear full accouterments but without pouches, on saddled horses with valises with greatcoats and flasks behind the saddle. Those without saddles are to leave their valises and flasks with their section baggage cart [*artel'naya povozka*], while the greatcoat is to be over the right shoulder, rolled along its whole length and tied at the ends with whitened straps."

e) "Entrenching tools (shovels and axes), when personnel are on foot, are to be worn on one's person in the manner of the infantry, but when mounted and on the move, then these are to be tied to the side of each ammunition caisson."

f) "As for noncombatants with horses (the bone setter [*konoprav*], nursing orderly, barber, smith, and farrier), they are to pack their greatcoats, valises, and water flasks the same way as combatants." (Illus. 1664.)

g) "Other noncombatants, except train personnel [*furleity*], have packed valises, water flasks, and greatcoats on their persons, on a strap 1 1/2 inches wide. This strap's ends fasten to iron buckles sewn onto the sides of the valise. It is to this same strap that the greatcoat, rolled into a tube the length of the valise, is tied by means of a loop sewn onto the top of the valise. The wooden water flask, wrapped in black leather, is fastened to the middle of the valise by a black leather strap across it. In this way the valise with greatcoat and flask is carried over the right shoulder, close to the back with the right end raised higher so that it lies somewhat diagonally." (Illus. 1665.)

h) Train personnel driving wagons leave their valises along with their greatcoats and flasks in their vehicles (112).

**10 March 1807**– **Canes** were withdrawn for officers and noncommissioned officers (113).

**22 September 1807**– With the disbandment of Horse-Artillery battalions and the distribution of their component companies to brigades, these companies were ordered to have **shoulder straps** of the following colors:

Horse company of the 2nd Brigade (Note: the Guard Artillery formed the 1st Brigade) – white, of the 3rd – white with red piping, of the 4th – yellow, of the 5th – yellow with red piping, of the 6th – black, of the 7th – light raspberry, of the 8th, light raspberry with black piping, of the 9th – turquoise, of the 10th turquoise with red piping, of the 11th – pink, of the 12th – pink with dark green piping, of the 13th – dark blue, of the 14th – red with black piping, of the 15th – white with black piping, of the 16th – dark green, of the 17th – dark green with red piping, of the 18th – dark blue with red piping, of the 21st – red, of the 22nd – black with red piping, of the Reserve St.-Petersburg Brigade – gray, of the Reserve Kiev Brigade – gray with red piping, and of the Reserve Moscow Brigade – lilac with red piping (114). (Note: The 19th, 20th, and 23rd Brigades did not have horse companies.)

**3 January 1808** – Lower ranks of all Horse Artillery companies were ordered to have just **red shoulder straps**, with the brigade number of yellow worsted cord sewn on, 1-3/4 inches [*1 vershok*] long, and when there was no number, then with the initial letters of the title, namely: in the St.-Petersburg Reserve Brigade – Cyrillic Р, in the Kiev Reserve Brigade – К, and in the Moscow Reserve Brigade – М. The acorn of the **sword knot** was ordered to be red and the loop and ring white (Illus. 1666). Field-grade officers were given **epaulettes** with a red cloth field and the brigade number in gold, similar to those established at this for field and company-grade officers of the Foot Artillery (Illus. 1666). Generals were directed to have epaulettes without numbers (115).

**19 February 1808**– For distinction shown against the French in 1807, the field and company-grade officers of Colonel Prince Yashvil's Horse-Artillery Company, 4th Artillery Brigade, and Colonel Yermolov's Horse-Artillery Company, 7th Artillery Brigade, were ordered to have **gold button loop embroidery** on their coats' collars and cuffs (Illus. 1666) (116).

**18 May 1808**– All combatant lower ranks in Horse-Artillery companies were ordered to have two **pistols** each (117).

**26 November 1808**– For all Horse-Artillery companies a new style of **crest** [*plyumazh*] was prescribed for their helmets, like that confirmed at this time for Cuirassier regiments. Officers were prescribed to have these crests only when on campaign, and the rest of the time to wear the previous thick style established 18 October 1803 (Illus. 1666) (118).

**11 February 1809**– All **noncombatant** lower ranks not possessing noncommissioned officer status were given a new pattern **forage cap**, identical to those established at this time for noncombatants in the Foot Artillery (119).

**4 April 1809**- **Noncommissioned officers** were ordered to have **galloon** not on the lower and side edges of the collar, but on the upper and side edges (120).

**8 June 1809**–The plumage on **generals' hats** was discontinued and the former pattern of buttonhole was replaced with a new one made of four thick, twisted cords, of which the two middle ones were intertwined with each other as if in a plait (121).

**28 August 1809**– Horse-Artillery officers were ordered to have **red cloth piping** not only along the top and sides of the coat collar, but also along the lower edge (Illus. 1667)(122).

**22 October 1809**– Lower ranks of the Horse Artillery were ordered to have **two shoulder straps** on their coats and greatcoats instead of just one (Illus. 1667) (123).

In this same year the **powdering of the hair** was completely discontinued for officers, and it was permitted for them when off duty to wear **frock coats** [*sertuki*] of the same pattern as established at this time for officers of the Foot Artillery. Also, **plumes** [*sultany*] on their hats were shortened. (124).

**25 October 1811**– Lower ranks of Horse-Artillery companies were given new **forage caps** [*furazhnyya shapki*] of the pattern introduced at this time in the Foot Artillery (Illus. 1668) (125).

**17 December 1811**- **Noncombatant lower ranks** of the Horse Artillery were given new uniforms identical to those received at this time by noncombatant lower ranks in the Foot Artillery(126).

**10 February 1812**– These lower ranks were ordered to have **shoulder straps** on their caftan coats [*kaftany*] and greatcoats of the same color and pattern as the shoulder straps of combatant ranks (127), and about this time there were the following changes in the uniforms of all combatant ranks of the Horse Artillery:

1) The thick [*gustoi*] style of **crest** on officers' helmets was completely abolished, leaving only the flat [*ploskii*] style.

2) The high **collars** which opened diagonally upwards were replaced by lower ones closed with small hooks (Illus. 1669).

3) Lower combatant ranks were given **gaiters** and officers **high boots** reaching up to the knees, the first having nine buttons (Illus. 1639).

4) Instead of the brigade number, it was ordered that **shoulder straps** and epaulettes were to have the company number and the initial letter of its title. For example, 1 K. in the 1st Horse Company [*1-ya Konnaya rota*] (128).

**29 November 1812**- In order to lessen their expenditures, Horse-Artillery officers were allowed to have stamped bronze [*kovanyi bronzovyi*] fittings to their **epaulettes** instead of gold, and white **sashes** and **sword knots** instead of silver (129).

**18 April 1813**– Horse Artillery Companies No. 3, 4, 6, and 12, were granted **badges** [*znaki*] for the helmet, with the inscription "For Distinction" ["*Za otlichie*"], following the style for Army Infantry regiments, i.e. in the form of a shield (Illus. 1670). Independently of these badges, officers of these companies were granted gold **embroidered button loops** on their coats' collars and cuffs, which was extended to other companies which would granted such a distinction (Illus. 1670 (130).

**20 May 1814**– The **gray riding trousers** with buttons and leather lining prescribed since 1802 for field and company-grade officers of Horse Artillery were replaced by likewise gray ones but with black cloth **double stripes** [*lampasy*] with red cloth piping, and without leather lining (Illus. 1670) (131).

**16 and 26 June 1814**– The following changes were made to the uniforms and weapons of combatant ranks in the Horse Artillery:

1) **Shakos** [*kivera*] were to be issued instead of helmets, of the same pattern as in the Foot Artillery except with the addition of hair plumes: for privates – white with black and orange at the base; for noncommissioned officers – white with black and orange at the top; for trumpeters – red; for field and company-grade officers – white with black and orange at the base (Illus. 1671 and 1672).

2) The double-breasted **coats** were changed to single-breasted, with nine buttons and red piping (Illus. 1671 and 1672).

3) White **pants** with high were replaced by long dark-green pants of the pattern described above for lancers, with double stripes, piping, and also buttons and red cords for fastening at the bottom (Illus. 1671 and 1672).

4) **Gloves** were kept only for officers and noncommissioned officers, for the former as before without cuffs [*krageny*], and for the latter with cuffs.

5) Broadswords [*palashi*] and wide sword belts with buckles were replaced by **sabers** [*sabli*] and sword belts with hooks, of the pattern for lancers. For lower ranks these sword belts were of whitened deerskin [*losinnyi*], while for officers they were black leather trimmed on the upper side with gold galloon (Illus. 1671 and 1672) (132).

**In 1814**, it was ordered that the **cockades** on officers' hats have white tape around them, later replaced by silver (Illus. 1673) (133).

**20 January 1816**– **Cuffs** on combatant ranks' coats were ordered to have dark-green flaps, in the style of the inf. (Illus. 1673) (134).

**10 February 1816**– Combatant lower ranks of the Horse Artillery were ordered to have shako **chinstraps** [*podvyaznye remni u kiverov*] with brass scales (135).

**16 November 1816**– The order of 28 August 1809 for officers in the Horse Artillery to have **red piping** all around the collar was extended to lower ranks (Illus 1673) (136).

**19 March 1817**– Noncommissioned officers of the Horse Artillery were ordered to have **gloves** without cuffs (137).

**22 September 1817**– All combatant ranks of Horse-Artillery companies were ordered to have **coats** of the pattern confirmed on 28 February 1817 for Dragoon regiments, i.e. with slit cuffs without flaps. When wearing the sash, officers were to have the coat with short tails and wear the same **pouches** as in Dragoon regiments, except with two gold crossed cannons and a gold single-flame grenade, instead of an eagle (Illus. 1674 and 1675) (138).

**27 November 1817**– The pale yellow cloth [*palevoe sukno*] of horse-artillery **shabracks** was ordered to be replaced by yellow [*zheltoe*] (139).

**5 October 1818**– Horse-Artillery companies of the **Separate Lithuania Corps** (Nos. 13 and 14) were given coats with black lapels (cloth for lower ranks, velvet for officers) piped red, and on the shakos, instead of plumes, there were to be pyramidal pompons [*piramidal'nye pompony*] the same color as the cords (Illus. 1676) (140).

**16 February 1819**– Horse-Artillery companies were ordered to have **covers** on the shakos, identical to those established at this time for Dragoon, Horse-Jäger, and Hussar regiments (141).

**20 February 1819**– In place of their hair plumes, these companies were given **pompons** of the pattern of 5 October 1818 for Horse-Artillery companies of the Separate Lithuania Corps (142).

**18 April 1820**– These **pompons** were discontinued (143).

**7 August 1820**– Generals assigned to the Horse-Artillery branch, and field and company-grade officers of the Horse Artillery, were allowed to wear **mustaches** (144).

**1 November 1820**– All combatant ranks of the Horse Arillery were ordered to have **red double stripes** on their riding trousers instead of black, as on the dark-green pants (Illus. 1677) (145). In this same year Horse-Artillery **trumpeters** began to sew their coats with chevrons placed more closely together than previously, as related above regarding musicians and drummers of the Foot Artillery (Illus. 1677) (146).

**27 January 1822**– Field and company-grade officers of the Horse Artillery were given **epaulettes** of a new pattern, identical to those received at this time by field and company-grade officers of the Foot Artillery (147).

**29 March 1825**- For combatant lower ranks, for faultless service, there were established **stripes** [*nashivki*] to be sewn on the left sleeve: for 10 years service - one, for 15 years - two, for 20 years - three; one over the other, all of yellow tape (148).

# X - GARRISON ARTILLERY (*GARNIZONNAYA ARTILLERIYA*)

**9 April 1801**- Lower ranks of the Garrison Artillery were ordered to cut off their **curls** and have **queues** only 7 inches long, tying them midway down the collar (149).

**10 May 1801**– **Officers** of Garrison Artillery were ordered to have the same uniforms as officers of Field Artillery except their hats did not have plumes or gold button-hole lace (Illus. 1678) (150).

**11 June 1801**– **Small clothes** for all combatant ranks of the Garrison Artillery, and in addition the gloves of officer candidates [*yunkera*] and fireworkers, were to be white instead of the previous light pale yellow [*svetlopalevyi*] (151).

**27 March 1802**– Personnel of the Garrison Artillery were prescribed the same uniforms as established on this date for the Field Foot Artillery but with **white buttons** instead of yellow (Illus 1679) and with different colored **shoulder straps**, which were:

  a) In the Rochensalm Company – red.

  b) In the Nikolaev, Akhtiar, and Kamenets-Podol'skii companies- white.

  c) In the Novodvinsk, Nyslott, Villmanstrand, Fredrikshamn, Kexholm, Viborg, St.-Petersburg, Kronstadt, Narva, Pskov, Velikie Luki, Shlüsselburg, Moscow, Kazan, Orenburg, Gurev, Tsaritsyn, Chernyi-Yar, Astrakhan, Yenotaevsk, Krasnyi-Yar, Kizlyar, and Mozdok commands – yellow.

  d) In the Kiev, Yelisavetgrad, Samara, Dmitrievsk, Ochakov, Kinburn, Tiraspol, Kherson, Taganrog, Azov, Yeisk, Petropavlovsk, (on the Sea of Azov), Aleksandrovsk, and Odessa commands – light raspberry.    e) In the Riga Citadel, Riga Town, Dünamünde, Pernau, Arensburg, Reval, Balic Port, Smolensk, and Tobolsk commands – pink.

  f) In the Selenginsk, Nerchinsk, Irkutsk, Zhelezinsk, Petropavlovsk (St. Peter Fortress), Omsk, Yamyshevsk, Biisk, Semipalatinsk, Ust-Kamenogorsk, and Petropavlovsk (in Kamchatka) commands – turquoise (152).

**Arsenal wardens** and **junior arsenal wardens** [*tseikhvartera i unter-tseikhvartera*] of the Garrison Artillery were also prescribed coats of the pattern established for the Foot Artillery but with dark-green cuffs and white buttons instead of yellow metal, the number of which on the cuff flaps was not three as for field artillerymen, but only two. They were authorized high sturdy boots [*botforty*] with spurs and officers' hats with a silver buttonhole loop, without a plume (Illus. 1680) (158).

**19 August 1803**– Instead of hats, lower ranks of the Garrison Artillery were given **cloth shakos** of the pattern introduced at this time in musketeer regiments and the Field Foot Artillery (Illus. 1681) (154).

**1 October 1806** – The **sheepskin warm coats** [*ovchinnyya fufaiki*] authorized for lower ranks were withdrawn (155).

**2 December 1806**– These same ranks were ordered to cut their **hair** short; generals, though, and field and company-grade officers, were in this regard allowed to proceed according to their personal wishes (156).     In this same year personnel in Garrison Artillery companies and commands were ordered to have **shoulder straps** according to the inspectorate to which they were assigned:

   a) In the St.-Petersburg and Finland Inspectorates – pale yellow.
   b) In the Lifland and Lithuania Inspectorates – white.
   c) In the Kiev and Taurica Inspectorates – red.
   d) On the Caucasian Line – raspberry.
   e) In the Siberia Inspectorate – pink.
   f) In all Arsenals – yellow.
   g) In powder works and laboratories [*porokhovye zavody i laboratorii*] – black (157).

   For privates the **pompons and tufts on shakos** were to be white with the center the same color as the shoulder strap, and white with black and orange for noncommissioned officers.

   For privates in Garrison companies and commands and at Arsenals, the acorn of the **sword knot** was to be the same color as the shoulder strap while all the rest of it was white; For noncommissioned officers the strap, fringe and loop were white, the acorn pale yellow, and the ring of three mixed colors: white, black, and orange.

   For privates in powder works and laboratories, the strap and acorn were black, and the loop and ring red. For noncommissioned officers the ring was white, black, and orange (158).

   **Master craftsmen** [*masterovye*] at all Arsenals, power works, and laboratories were prescribed the same uniforms as noncombatants in the Foot Field Artillery, except their frock coats [*sertuki*] were a little longer and the skirts not turned back (Illus. 1682). For work, they had a coat that was even longer, of gray cloth, with two rows of covered buttons and a turned down collar (Illus. 1683).

   **Powder workers** [*porokhovshchiki*], when processing gunpowder, were ordered to be in leather jackets [*kurtki*] and pants, tied at the wrists, waist, and under the calves with cords. On the head was to be worn a leather headdress [*shapka*] into which were inserted clear glass goggles [*belye stekla*] in a brass frame. This head covering, like the jacket, was tied in back with narrow leather thongs (Illus. 1684) (159).

**10 March 1807**– **Canes** were withdrawn for officers and noncommissioned officers (160).

**17 January 1808**– Generals, field and company-grade officers, and lower ranks of Garrison Artillery companies and commands were ordered to have black **shoulder straps**, while personnel at Arsenals, powder works, and laboratories were to have yellow (161).

**12 August 1808** – Officers and lower ranks of the newly established **Mobile arsenals** [*Podvizhnye arsenaly*] were prescribed all the same uniform clothing, accouterments, and weaponry as laid down for Permanent arsenals, except buttons and galloon lace were to be yellow (162).

**15 August 1808**– **Fireworkers** [*Feierverkery*, i.e. sergeants] at all Arsenals were ordered to have coats with a single row of buttons (163).

**In this same year** there were the following innovations for lower ranks throughout the Garrison Artillery:

   a) In place of the the shakos established in 1803 – *kiver* **shakos** similar to those described above for the Field Foot Artillery, with a red pompon (Illus. 1685).
   b) Winter **pants** with leather leggings and seven white (tin) buttons, and for summer—pants with integral spats (Illus. 1685).
   c) **Sword belts** over the shoulder, with straight short swords [*tesaki*] (Illus. 1685) (164).

**12 November 1808**– When not on duty, field and company-grade officers were allowed to wear dark-green cloth **pants** instead of white ones (165).

**22 November 1808**– Generals and field and company-grade officers of the Garrison Artillery (including Arsenals, powder works, and laboratories) were given **epaulettes** in place of shoulder straps, of the pattern established on 3 January of this year for the Field Artillery, except with a black or yellow cloth field, according to the color of the lower ranks' shoulder straps (Illus. 1686) (166).

**8 June 1809**–The plumage on **generals' hats** was discontinued and the former pattern of buttonhole was replaced with a new one made of four thick, twisted cords, of which the two middle ones were intertwined with each other as if in a plait (Illus. 1686) (167).

**17 October 1809**– Combatant lower ranks throughout the Garrison Artillery were ordered to have **yellow buttons** on the leggings on the lower part of their pants, instead of white (168).

**25 December 1809**– Generals and officers of this same Artillery branch were allowed to wear **frock coats** [*sertuki*] when off duty, of the same style as used at this time by Generals and officers of the Field Foot Artillery (169).

**25 October 1811**– Lower ranks of the Garrison Artillery were given new **forage caps** [*furazhnyya shapki*] of dark-green cloth with a black band, of the same pattern as the caps on 23 October [sic – should be September – M.C.] of this year in Grenadier and other Army Infantry regiments and in the Field Artillery, but with the following differences in color:

   In Garrison companies – black piping around the top of the cap, and the company number in red cord on the front of the band (Illus. 1687, a).

   In Laboratory companies – black piping around the top of the cap, and a number on the band in yellow cord (Illus. 1687, b).

   In fortress commands – without piping and without a number (Illus. 1687, c).

   In powder works detachments – yellow piping on the upper edge of the band and a yellow letter on the band (Cyrillic O for Okhtensk, Cyrillic SH for Shostensk, and Cyrillic K for Kazan) (Illus. 1687, d).

   In detachments at Permanent arsenals – yellow piping around the top of the cap and a yellow letter on the band (Cyrillic P for St. Petersburg, Cyrillic M for Moscow, Cyrillic B for Bryansk, and Cyrillic K for Kiev) (Illus. 1687, e).   In detachments at Mobile arsenals – yellow piping around the top of the cap (Illus. 1687, f).

   In Replacement parks [*Zapasnye parki*] – gray piping around the top of the cap (Illus. 1687, g) (170).

**11 December 1811**– Combatant lower ranks [sic – should be **noncombatant** – M.C.] throughout the Garrison Artillery, except laboratory companies (who kept their frock coats with a single row of buttons), were given **new uniforms** in place of the ones in use since 1802. These were identical to those established at this time for noncombatant lower ranks of the Field Foot Artillery (171).

**10 February 1812**– These ranks were ordered to have **shoulder straps** on their caftan coats [*kaftany*] and greatcoats of the same color and pattern as the shoulder straps of combatant ranks (172), and about this time there were the following changes in the uniforms of combatant ranks of the Garrison Artillery:

   1) New-pattern **shakos** were issued, lower than before, with a big indentation or widening upwards, and sloping upwards at the sides. They lacked the sewn-on neck or ear flaps which from this time on were worn separately (Illus. 1688).

   2) The high **collars** which opened diagonally upwards were replaced by lower ones closed with small hooks (Illus. 1688).

   3) Lower combatant ranks were given **gaiters** and officers **high boots** reaching up to the knees, the first having nine buttons (Illus. 1688).

   4) Noncombatant lower ranks of **laboratory companies** were ordered to have **collars** on their frock coats and greatcoats of the same pattern as for combatant ranks (173).

**24 January 1816**– **Scabbards** for short swords [*tesaki*] and officers' swords [*shpagi*] were ordered to be black throughout the Garrison Artillery, and about this time officers of this branch were began to wear hats with white (later silver) ribbon around the **cockade**, after the example of officers in the Field Artillery and other arms (174).

**8 August 1817**- The size of the **forage cap** was fixed as established at this time for forage caps in Army infantry regiments (175).

**26 September 1817** – The description confirmed on this day for **shakos** and **accouterments** in the army infantry and the rules for wearing them were also adopted in the Garrison Artillery (176).

**8 December 1817**- The leather **gaiters** or **leggings** [*kragi*] on the cloth pants were ordered to have **integral spats** [*kozyrki*] of a pattern similar to the gaiter spats [*shtibletnye kozyrki*] of summer pants (177).

**17 February 1818**– The Garrison Artillery was ordered to have **red piping** all around the collar (Illus. 1689) (178).

**March 1819**– Lower ranks of the Garrison Artillery were ordered to have company numbers and initial letters of arsenal and powder works on the **shoulder strap**, in red cord on black shoulder straps and in black cord on yellow straps. For officers the **epaulette** field was left without numbers (179).

**20 April 1820**– The following **uniforms** were confirmed for lower ranks in the **Garrison Artillery**:

   a) In Garrison Artillery companies – dark-green coat with two rows of buttons, red piping, dark-green pants, black shoulder straps piped red and with a yellow nuber, *kiver* shako of the previous pattern, white buttons (Illus. 1690).   b)

In Mobile arsenals – dark-green coat with a single row of buttons, red piping, dark-green pants, yellow shoulder straps, *kiver* shako of the previous pattern, yellow buttons (Illus. 1691).     c) In Permanent arsenals - dark-green frock coat with a single row of buttons, red piping, dark-green pants, yellow shoulder straps, dark-green forage cap with black band, visor, red piping, and yellow initial letter; white buttons (Illus. 1692).     d) In Laboratory companies - dark-green coat with a single row of buttons, without piping, dark-green pants, dark-green forage cap with black band, visor, red piping, and a yellow number; white buttons (Illus. 1693) (180).

**2 May 1822**– Officers of the Garrison Artillery were given gray **riding trousers** with black double stripes and red piping, which were ordered to be worn on the same basis as related above for 16 April 1816 regarding officers of the Field Foot Artillery (Illus. 1694) (181).

**14 May 1824**– Combatant lower ranks of Artillery garrisons were ordered to have on their **shakos**, instead of a cockade, the same **plate** as in the Field Artillery, but of of white tin. Officers were given a shako of the same pattern but with silver cords and pompon (Illus. 1695 and 1696) (182).

**29 March 1825**- For combatant lower ranks who had been transferred to the Garrison Artillery from the Guards or Army because of wounds or other disabilities, there were established **stripes** [*nashivki*] for faultless service, of yellow tape, identical to, and worn on the same basis as, those described above for the Field Artillery (183).

*

# NOTES

(1) Complete Collection of Laws of the Russian Empire [*Polnoe Sobranie Zakonov Rossiiskoi Imperii*, hereafter *PSZ*], Vol. XXVI, pg. 609. No. 19,826.

(2) Ibid., Vol. XLIV, Pt. II, Directives on uniforms, pg. 28, No. 19,863.

(3) Ibid., No. 19,867; information received from the Commissariat Department of the War Ministry; statements by contemporaries.

(4) Correspondence from the Commissariat Office to the Inspector of All Artillery, dated 11 June 1801.

(5) PSZ, Vol. XLIV, pg. 25, No. 20,201, and information received from the Commissariat Department of the War Ministry.

(6) Ibid., pg. 30, No. 20,485, and information received from the same Department.

(7) Ibid., Vol. XLIV, pg. 28, No. 20,201.

(8) Ibid., Vol. XXVIII, pg. 415, No. 21,377, information received from the Commissariat Department of the War Ministry.

(9) Ibid., pg. 67, No. 20,987.

(10) HIGHEST confirmed table of uniform items and accouterments: a Field Artillery regiment and musicians authorized for the 1st Field Artillery Regiment, 27 December 1803; issued in 1807: drawings depicting various views of clothing and other accouterments for artillery crews under the control of the Inspector of All Artillery, Graf Arakcheev, and actual items preserved in various Arsenals and at the Commissariat Department of the War Ministry.

(11) Information received from the same Department, and contemporary drawings and coats.

(12) See above, in the entry for 16 June 1803.

(13) Table for a Field Artillery regiment, referenced above in Note 10.

(14) PSZ, Vol. XLIV, pg. 29, No 20,109.

(15) Ibid., pg. 25, No 20,201, and description accompanying the drawings referenced above in Note 10.

(16) HIGHEST confirmed table: number of tools to be kept in one Field Artillery regiment, 17 December 1803.

(17) Information received from the Commissariat Department of the War Ministry; the drawings referenced above in Note 10; the description accompanying these drawings, pg. 5, and actual pouches preserved in Arsenals.

(18) HIGHEST confirmed table of uniforms, accouterments, and weapons of an Artillery Pontoon regiment, 16 March 1805; and PSZ Vol. XLIV, Pt. II, addendum of Section One, pg. 29, No 21,665.

(19) PSZ, Vol. XLIV, pg. 67, No. 21,969.

(20) Ibid., pg. 28, No. 22,009.

(21) Ibid., pg. 31, No. 22,197.

(22) Information received from the Commissariat Department of the War Ministry.

(23) PSZ, Vol. XXIX, pg. 201, No. 22,382.

(24) Information received from the Commissariat Department of the War Ministry, and the drawings referenced above in Note 10, and the description accompanying these drawings, pgs. 2, 3, and 8.

(25) Information received from the Commissariat Department of the War Ministry.

(26) Information received from that same place and correspondence from the Government Military Collegium to the Commissariat Office, 22 September 1807.

(27) Information received from that Department.

(28) Ibid.

(29) Information received from that same place, and PSZ, Vol. XLIV, pg. 67, No. 22,727.

(30) Information received from that Department; PSZ, XLIV, pg. 27, No. 22,740; actual epaulettes preserved up to now.

(31) Ibid.

(32) Ibid.

(33) War Ministry's Chancellery Archive, in the collection of orders signed by the Sovereign, Book 156, pg. 627.

(34) Information received from the Commissariat Department of the War Ministry.

(35) PSZ, Vol. XLIV, pg. 27, No. 22,881.

(36) Archive of the War Ministry's Inspection Department, material relating to the Minister of War's proposal, with drawings and description, of the manner in which to wear knapsacks and greatcoats, 1808, No. 13786/654, and statements by contemporaries.

(37) War Ministry's Chancellery Archive, in a collection of HIGHEST directives, Book 157, pg. 940.

(38) PSZ, Vol. XLIV, pg. 27, No. 23,303.

(39) Ibid., pg. 67, No. 23,335.

(40) Ibid., Vol. , pg. 663, No. 23,343.

(41) Information received from the Commissariat Department of the War Ministry.

(42) PSZ, Vol. , pg. 781, No. 23,478, and model shako preserved at the Commissariat Department of the War Ministry.

(43) Information received from that Department.

(44) PSZ, Vol. , pg. 950, No. 23,625; information received from that Department, and an actual model knapsack preserved there.

(45) PSZ, Vol. , pg. 965, No. 23,654.

(46) PSZ, Vol. , pg. 1006, No. 25,695.

(47) Ibid., Vol. XLIV, pg. 31, No. 2373, and model shako cords preserved by the Commissariat Department of the War Ministry.

(48) Information received from that Department..

(49) PSZ, Vol. XLIV, pg. 27, No. 23,810.

(50) Ibid., No. 23,897.

(51) Ibid., Vol. , pg. 1362, No. 24,019, and actual shakos from that time, preserved up to now.

(52) Information received from the Commissariat Department of the War Ministry; evidence from contemporaries and hats and frock coats preserved up to now.

(53) Ditto.

(54) PSZ, Vol. I, pg. 362, No. 24,367.

(55) Ibid., pg. 517, No. 24,488, and model shako cords preserved by the Commissariat Department of the War Ministry.

(56) PSZ, Vol. XLIV, pg. 217, No. 24,829.

(57) Ditto.

(58) Ditto.

(59) Ditto.

(60) PSZ, Vol. XLIV, pg. 31, No.No. 24,911 and 24,912, and model uniforms preserved by the Commissariat Department of the War Ministry.

(61) PSZ, Vol. XLIV, pg. 70, No. 24,991.

(62) Information received from the Commissariat Department of the War Ministry and model items preserved there, and items preserved in various Arsenals and by private persons.

(63) PSZ, Vol. II, pg. 555, No. 25,370, a.

(64) Ibid.

(65) Information received from the Commissariat Department of the War Ministry and evidence from contemporaries.

(66) Ditto.

(67) PSZ, Vol. III, pg. 450, No. 20,095, and information received from the Commissariat Department of the War Ministry;.

(68) Information received from that same Department.

(69) HIGHEST resolution on a report by the head of the War Ministry, 13 April 1814.

(70) PSZ, Vol. III, pg. 907, No. 26,322.

(71) Information received from the Commissariat Department of the War Ministry.

(72) Ditto.

(73) PSZ, Vol. XLIV, pg. 104, No. 26, 992, and information received from the Commissariat Department of the War Ministry.

(74) Ibid., No. 27,067, and information received from the Commissariat Department of the War Ministry.

(75) Information received from that same Department.

(76) PSZ, Vol. XLIV, pg. 117, No. 27,275.

(77) Ibid., pg. 137, No. 27,392, and model uniforms preserved by the Commissariat Department of the War Ministry.

(78) Ibid., pg. 121, No. 27,504, and information received from the Commissariat Department of the War Ministry.

(79) PSZ, Vol. XLIV, pg. 108, No. 27,653.

(80) Ibid., pg. 120, and information received from the Commissariat Department of the War Ministry.

(81) Order of the Chief of H.I.M.'s Main Staff, 4 April 1819, No. 21.

(82)Information received from the Commissariat Department of the War Ministry.

(83) PSZ, Vol. XLIV, pg. 118, No. 27,971, and information received from the Commissariat Department of the War Ministry.

(84) Information received from the same Department.

(85) Order of the Chief of H.I.M.'s Main Staff, 4 June 1820, No. 32.

(86) Information received from the Commissariat Department of the War Ministry.

(87) Ditto.

(88) Ditto.

(89) PSZ, Vol. XLIV, pg. 119, No. 28,895.

(90) Ibid., pg. 122, No. 26,658.

(91) Order to the Separate Corps of Military Settlements, 16 January 1824, No. 22, and information received from the Commissariat Department of the War Ministry.

(92) PSZ, Vol. XL, pg. 188, No. 30,309.

(93) Ibid., Vol. XLIV, pg. 609, No. 19,826.

(94) Ibid., Vol. XLIV, pg. 28, No. 19,863.

(95) Ibid., No. 19,867.

(96) Ibid., No. 19898.

(97) Correspondence of the Commissariat Office to the Inspector of All Artillery.

(98) PSZ, Vol. XLIV, pg. 25, No. 20,201.

(99) Ibid., pg. 30, No. 20,485.

(100) Ibid., pg. 28, No. 20,201.

(101) Memorandum from the Government Military Collegium to the Military Commission, dated 22 June 1803.

(102) PSZ, Vol., XVII, pg. 834, No. 20,989.

(103) HIGHEST confirmed table of uniforms, accouterments, and weapons for a Horse-Artillery battalion, 27 December 1803; also, the drawings and actual items referenced above in Note 10.

(104) Information received from the Commissariat Department of the War Ministry, and contemporary drawings and coats.

(105) See above in the entry for 16 June 1803.

(106) Table, op.cit., Note 103.

(107) PSZ, Vol. XLIV, pg. 29, No. 20,109.

(108) HIGHEST confirmed tables: one referenced above in Note 103, and another, confirmed by HIGHEST authority on 27 December 1803, on how many implements to be kept in one Horse-Artillery battalion.

(109) PSZ, Vol. XLIV, pg. 31, No. 22, 197.

(110) Information received from the Commissariat Department of the War Ministry.

(111) PSZ, Vol. XXIX, pg. 201, No. 22,382.

(112) Information received from the Commissariat Department of the War Ministry; the drawings referenced above in Note 10, and the description accompanying these drawings, pgs. 9-14.

(113) Information received from the Commissariat Department of the War Ministry.

(114) Ditto.

(115) Information received from the same Department, and PSZ, Vol. XLIV, pg. 27, No. 22,740.

(116) Ibid., pg. 28, No. 22,832.

(117) Ibid., Vol. XX, pg. 263, No. 23,029.

(118) Ibid., Vol. XLIV, pg. 54, No. 23,373.

(119) Ibid., Vol. , pg. 781, No. 23,478.

(120) Information received from the Commissariat Department of the War Ministry.

(121) PSZ, Vol. , pg. 1006, No. 23,695.

(122) Ibid., Vol. XLIV, pg. 27, No. 23,810.

(123) Ibid., pg. 28, No. 23,925.

(124) Information received from the Commissariat Department of the War Ministry, and evidence from contemporaries.

(125) PSZ, Vol. XLIV, pg. 27, No. 24,829.

(126) Ibid., pg. 31, No.No. 24,911 and 24,912, and information received from the Commissariat Department of the War Ministry.

(127) PSZ, Vol. XLIV, pg. 70, No. 24,991.

(128) Information received from the Commissariat Department of the War Ministry.

(129) PSZ, Vol. XLLIV, pg. 50, No. 25,278.

(130) HIGHEST Order, 13 April 1813, and information received from the Commissariat Department of the War Ministry.

(131) Information received from the same Department.

(132) Information received from the same Department, and PSZ, Vol. XLII, Pt. II, addendum to Section One, pg. 2, No. 25,607. Shako plumes, prescribed by the table to be black, did not follow that and were directly issued white.

(133) Information received from the Commissariat Department of the War Ministry, and evidence from contemporaries.

(134) Ditto.

(135) Ditto.

(136) Ditto.

(137) PSZ, Vol. XLIV, pg. 102, No. 26,739.

(138) Ibid., pg. 119, No. 27061.

(139) Ibid., No. 27,166.

(140) PSZ, Vol. XLIV, pg. 137, No. 27,592, and information received from the Commissariat Department of the War Ministry.

(141) Ibid., No. 27,554.

(142) Ibid., pg. 134, No. 28,153.
(143) Ibid., pg. 122, No. 28,240.
(144) Ibid., Vol. VII, pg. 409, No. 28,374.
(145) Ibid., Vol. XLIV, pg. 119, No. 28,459.
(146) Information received from the Commissariat Department of the War Ministry.
(147) PSZ, Vol. XLIV, pg. 119, No. 28,895.
(148) Ibid., Vol. XL, pg. 188, No. 30,309.
(149) Ibid., Vol.. XLIV, pg. 609, No. 19,826.
(150) Ibid., Vol. XLIV, pg. 28, No. 19,863.
(151) Memorandum from the Commissariat Office to the Inspector of All Artillery, 11 June 1801.
(152) PSZ, Vol. XLIV, pgs. 25 and 26, No. 20,201.
(153) Ibid., pg. 26.
(154) Information received from the Commissariat Department of the War Ministry.
(155) Ditto.
(156) PSZ, Vol. XXIX, pg. 201, No. 22,382.
(157) Information received from the Commissariat Department of the War Ministry, and the drawings referenced above in Note 10, and the the description accompanying them, pg. 16.
(158) Ditto.
(159) Ditto.
(160) Information received from the same Department.
(161) PSZ, Vol. XLIV, pg. 29, No. 22,759.
(162) Ibid., Vol. XLIII, Pt. II, book of authorization tables from 1801 through 1805, pg. 96, No. 23,218.
(163) Ibid., Vol. , pg. 525, No. 23,225.
(164) Information received from the Commissariat Department of the War Ministry.
(165) Ditto.
(166) Information received from the same Department, and PSZ, Vol. XLIV, pg. 29, No. 23,367.
(167) Ibid., Vol. , pg. 1006, No. 23,695.
(168) Ibid., Vol. XLIV, pg. 24, No. 23,914.
(169) Information received from the Commissariat Department of the War Ministry.
(170) PSZ, Vol. XLIV, pg. 27, No. 24,829.
(171) Ibid., pg. 31, No.No. 24,911 and 24,912, and information received from the Commissariat Department of the War Ministry.
(172) Ibid., pg. 70, No. 24,991.
(173) Information received from the Commissariat Department of the War Ministry.
(174) Ditto.
(175) Ditto.
(176) Ditto.
(177) Ditto.
(178) PSZ, Vol. XLIV, pg. 117, No. 27,275.
(179) Information received from the Commissariat Department of the War Ministry.
(180) Ditto.
(181) PSZ, Vol. XLIV, pg. 119, No. 29,626.
(182) Ibid., pg. 139, No. 29,912.
(183) Ibid., Vol. XL, pg. 188, No. 30,309.

# РИСУНКИ

## ОДЕЖДЫ и ВООРУЖЕНІЯ

### РОССІЙСКИХЪ

### ВОЙСКЪ.

# PLATES LIST OF ILLUSTRATIONS

1650. Shako plate for Grenadier Artillery Brigades, 1820-1828.

1651. Drummer. Foot Field Artillery, 1820-1825.

1652. Cannoneers. Grenadier Artillery Brigades, 1824-1825.

1653. Bombardier and Company-grade Officer. Horse Artillery, 1801.

1654. Cannoneer. Horse Artillery, 1802-1803.

1655. Private. Horse Artillery, 1803-1806.

1656. Private. Horse Artillery, 1804-1806.

1657. Bombardiers. Horse Artillery, 1804-1808.

1658. Noncommissioned Officer. Horse Artillery, 1804-1807.

1659. Trumpeter and Staff-Trumpeter. Horse Artillery, 1804-1807.

1660. Company-grade Officers and General. Horse Artillery, 1804-1807.

1661. Private. Horse Artillery, 1804-1807.

1662. Private. Horse Artillery, 1806-1807.

1663. Noncommissioned Officer. Horse Artillery, 1806-1807.

1664. Barber and Bonesetter. Horse Artillery, 1806-1809.

1665. Medical Assistant [Fel'dsher]. Horse Artillery, 1806-1807.

1666. Field-grade Officer and Cannoneer. Horse Artillery, 1808-1809.

1667. Company-grade Officer and Bombardier. Horse Artillery, 1809-1811.

1668. Privates. Horse Artillery, 1811.

1669. Noncommissioned Officer and Field-grade Officer. Horse Artillery, 1812-1813.

1670. Field-grade Officer and Private. Horse Artillery, 1814.

1671. Bombardier and Trumpeter. Horse Artillery, 1814-1816.

1672. Field-grade Officers. Horse Artillery, 1814-1816. (One of the field-grade officers is shown with button loops on the coat and with a Badge for Distinction on the shako.)

1673. Company-grade Officer and Cannoneer. Horse Artillery, 1816.

1674. Company-grade Officers. Horse Artillery, 1817-1819.

1675. Pouch for Horse-Art. Officers, established in 1817. (Note: Later, about 1821, the belt for the pouch began to be fastened no longer by rings, but in the same manner as belts for inf. pouches, as shown below in Plate No. 1708.)

1676. Field-grade Officer and Bombardier. Horse Artillery of the Lithuania Corps, 1818-1825.

1677. Trumpeter and Company-grade Officer. Horse Artillery. 1820-1825.

1678. Officer. Garrison Artillery, 1801-1802.

1679. Company-grade Officer, Noncommissioned Officer, and Private. Garrison Artillery, 1802-1803.

1680. Arsenal Warden [Tseikhvarter]. Garrison Artillery, 1802-1804.

1681. Noncommissioned Officer and Private. Garrison Artillery, 1803-1806.

1682. Master Craftsmen [Masterovye]. Powder Works, 1806-1807.

1683. Master Craftsmen. Powder Works, 1806-1811. (In working uniform.)

1684. Powder Workers [Porokhovshchiki]. Powder Works. (In working dress.)

1685. Arsenal Fireworker and Private. Garrison Artillery Companies, 1808-1809.

1686. General. Garrison Artillery, 1808-1809.

1687. Forage caps for lower ranks in the Garrison Artillery, established 25 October 1811. a) Garrison companies. b) Laboratory companies. c) Fortress Commands. d) Detachments at Powder Works. e) Detachments at Permanent Arsenals. f) Detachments at Mobile Arsenals. g) Replacement Parks.

1688. Company-grade Officer and Private. Garrison Artillery, 1812-1816.

1689. Noncommissioned Officer and Company-grade Officer. Garrison Artillery, 1818-1819.

1690. Company-grade Officer, Cannoneer, and Drummer. Garrison Artillery, 1820-1824.

1691. Company-grade Officer and Noncommissioned Officer. Mobile Arsenals, 1820-1824.

1692. Noncommissioned Officer. Permanent Arsenals, 1820-1825.

1693. Private. Laboratory Companies, 1820-1825.

1694. Company-grade Officer. Garrison Artillery, 1822-1825.

1695. Private and Field-grade Officer. Garrison Artillery, 1824-1825.

1696. Drummer. Garrison Artillery, 1824-1825.

*Cannoneers [i.e. artillery privates - M.C.]. Foot Artillery 1801*

*General. Foot Artillery, 1801*

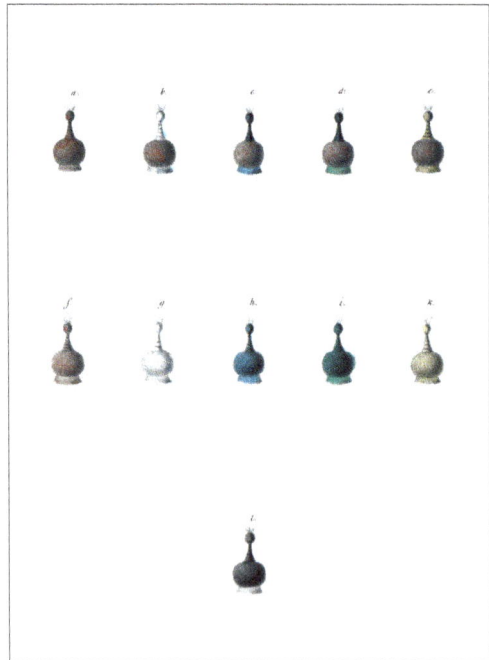

*Officer's shabrack and holsters, Foot Artillery, established in 1803 - Company and Field-grade Officers' epaulettes, Foot Artillery, 1808-1821*

*Sword knots for lower ranks of the Foot Artillery, established in 1819 - Shako plate for Grenadier Artillery Brigades, 1820-1828*

*Mounted Gun Handler and Cannoneers. Foot Artillery, 1803-1805*

*Bombardier [i.e. artillery corporal - M.C.]. Foot Artillery, 1803-1807*

*Fireworker [i.e. artillery noncommissioned officer - M.C.]. Foot Artillery, 1803-1807*

*Company and Battalion Drummers. Foot Artillery, 1803-1807.*

1610

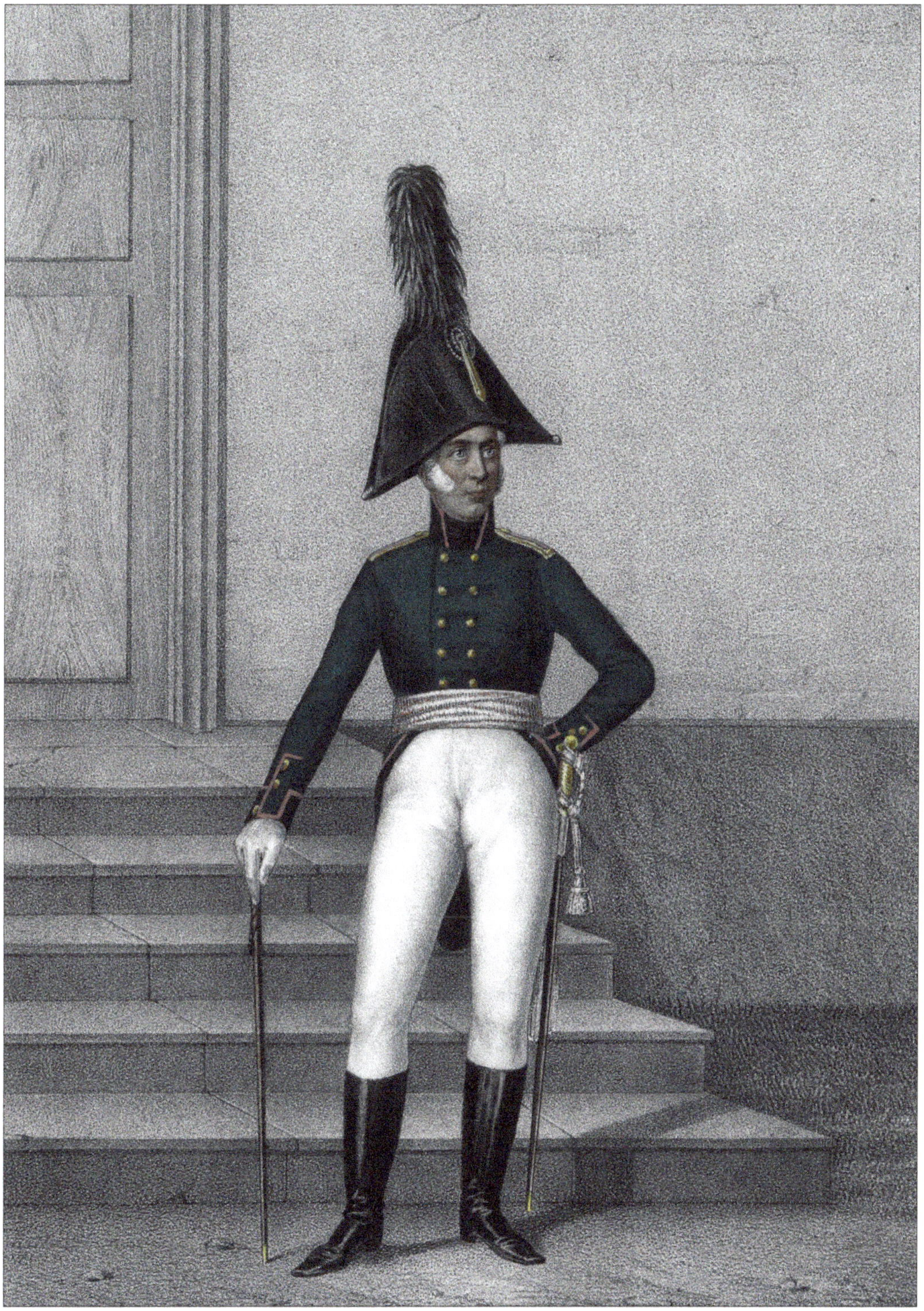

*Company-grade Officer. Foot Artillery, 1803-1807*

Company-grade Officer of the Train. Foot Artillery, 1803-1807

*Train Noncommissioned Officer and Clerk. Foot Artillery, 1803-1807*

*Barber. Foot Artillery, 1803-1807*

*Train Privates. Foot Artillery, 1803-1807*

*Pontoniers. Pontoon Regiment (2nd and 3rd Class), 1805-1807*

*Pontonier 1st Class and Noncommissioned Officer. Pontoon Regiment, 1805-1807*

*Company-grade Officer and Clerk. Pontoon Regiment, 1805-1807*

*Company-grade Officer. Foot Artillery of the Caucasus Inspectorate, 1806-1807*

Cannoneer. Foot Artillery, 1806-1807

1620

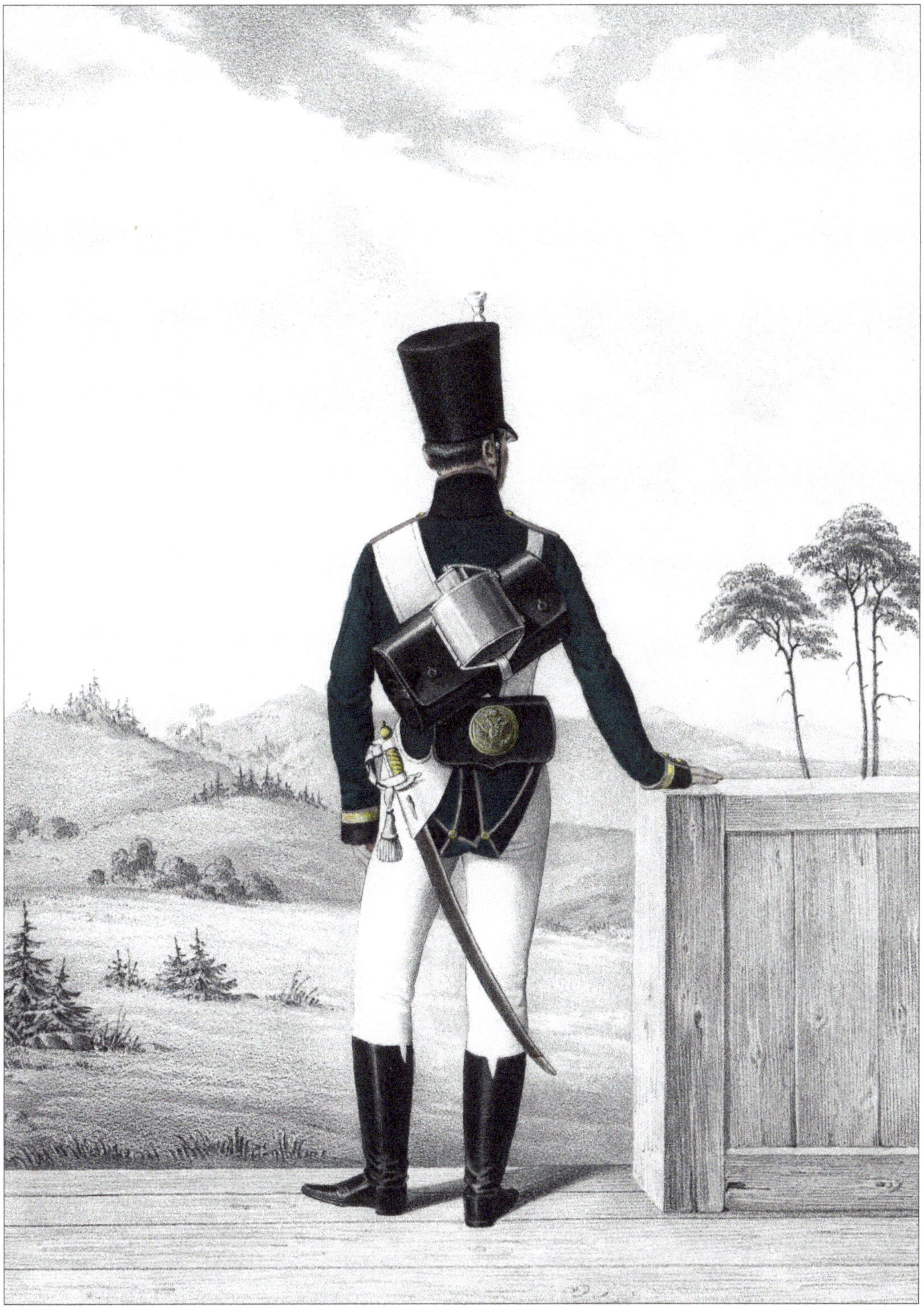

*Bombardier. Foot Artillery, 1806-1807*

Mounted Cannoneer. Foot Artillery, 1806-1807

*Mounted Cannoneer. Foot Artillery, 1806-1807*

*Bombardier and Gun Handler. Foot Artillery, 1806-1807*

*1624*

*Noncombatant Noncommissioned Officer. Foot Artillery, 1806-1807*

*Barber and Master Craftsman. Foot Artillery, 1806-1807*

*Cannoneer and Company-grade Officer. Foot Artillery, 1808.*

*Noncommissioned Officer. Potoon Companies, 1808*

*Company-grade Officer. Foot Artillery. (With lace button loops and in campaign uniform.) 1808-1809*

Bombardiers. Foot Artillery, 1808-1809

*Noncombatant. Foot Artillery, 1809*

*Noncommissioned Officer. Foot Artillery, 1809-1810*

*Company Drummer and Noncommissioned Officer. Foot Artillery, 1809-1811*

*Company-grade Officers and Mounted Gun Handler. Foot Artillery, 1809-1811*

*Noncommissioned Officer. Foot Artillery, 1811*

Privates. Foot Artillery, 1811

*Noncombatants. Foot Artillery, 1811*

*Field-grade Officer and Noncommissioned Officer. Foot Artillery, 1812-1816*

*Field-grade Officer. Foot Artillery. (With lace button loops and badge for distinction on the shako.) 1813-1814*

Company-grade Officer. Foot Artillery, 1814-1816

*Drum Major and Drummer. Foot Artillery, 1815-1816*

*Bombardier. Grenadier Artillery Brigades, 1816*

*Cannoneers. Field and Grenadier Brigades of Foot Artillery, 1817-1819*

*Cannoneer. Foot Field Brigades of the Artillery of the Lithuania Corps, 1818-1823*

*Company-grade Officer. Foot Field Brigades of the Artillery of the Lithuania Corps, 1818-1825*

*Drummers. Grenadier and Field Brigades of Foot Artillery, 1818-1820 Drummers. Grenadier and Field Brigades of Foot Artillery, 1818-1820*

1649

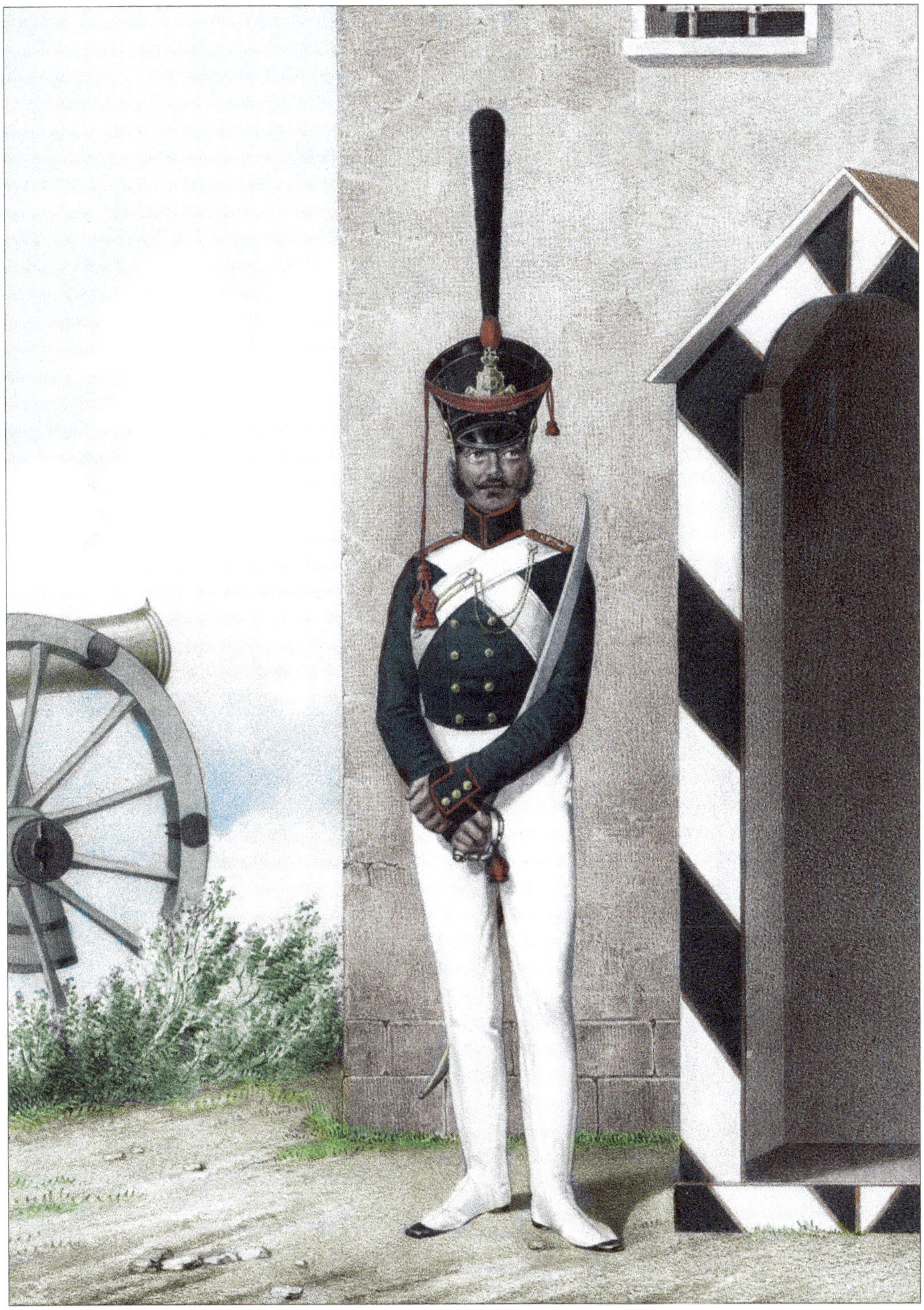

*Cannoneer. Grenadier Artillery Brigades, 1820-1823*

*Drummer. Foot Field Artillery, 1820-1825*

*Cannoneers. Grenadier Artillery Brigades, 1824-1825*

*Bombardier and Company-grade Officer. Horse Artillery, 1801*

*Cannoneer. Horse Artillery, 1802-1803*

1655

*Private. Horse Artillery, 1803-1806*

*Private. Horse Artillery, 1804-1806*

*Bombardiers. Horse Artillery, 1804-1808*

*Noncommissioned Officer. Horse Artillery, 1804-1807*

*Trumpeter and Staff-Trumpeter. Horse Artillery, 1804-1807*

*Company-grade Officers and General. Horse Artillery, 1804-1807*

*Private. Horse Artillery, 1804-1807*

*Private. Horse Artillery, 1806-1807*

*Noncommissioned Officer. Horse Artillery, 1806-1807*

*Barber and Bonesetter. Horse Artillery, 1806-1809*

*Medical Assistant [Fel′dsher]. Horse Artillery, 1806-1807*

*Field-grade Officer and Cannoneer. Horse Artillery, 1808-1809*

*Company-grade Officer and Bombardier. Horse Artillery, 1809-1811*

1668

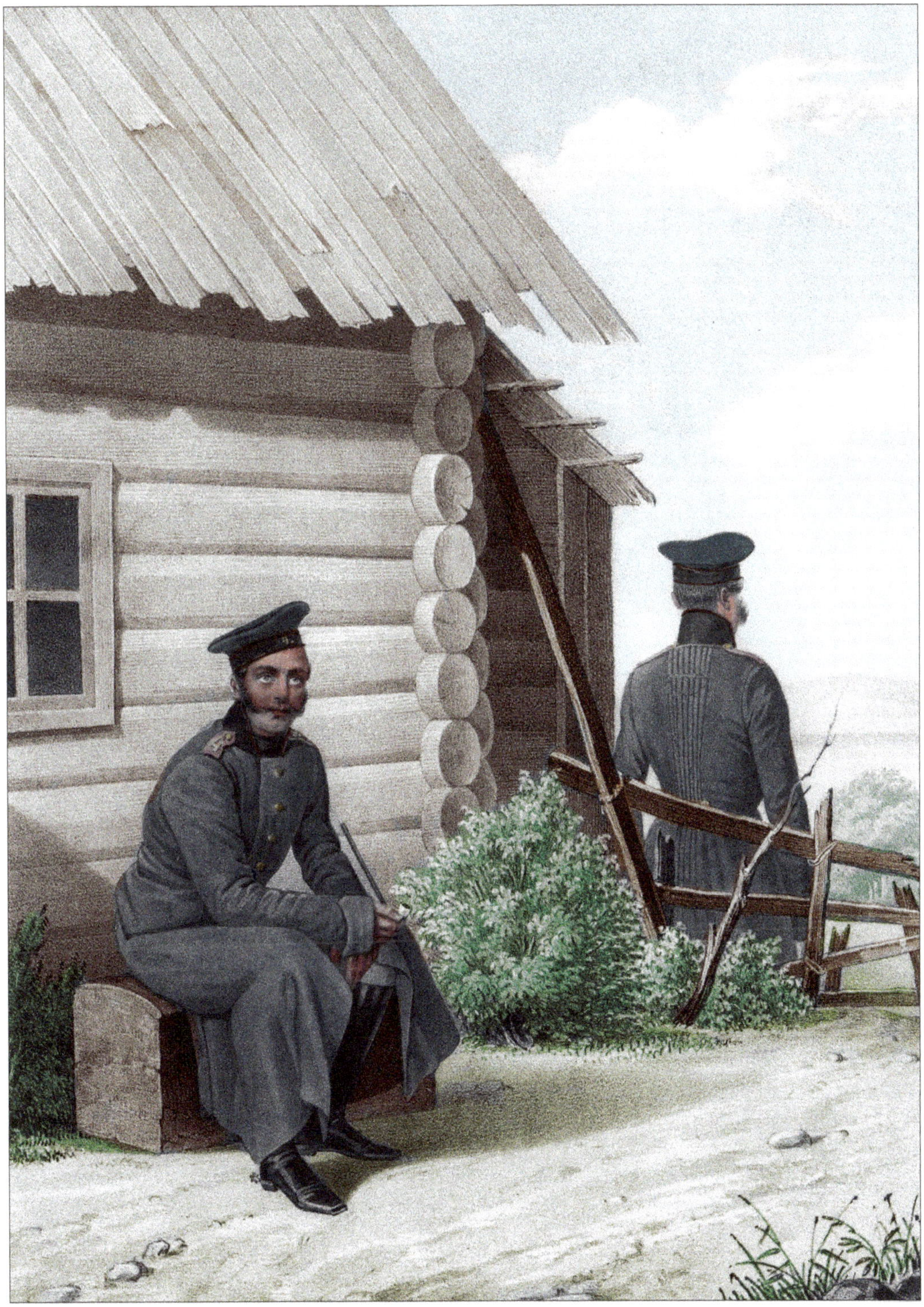

Privates. Horse Artillery, 1811

*Noncommissioned Officer and Field-grade Officer. Horse Artillery, 1812-1813*

*Field-grade Officer and Private. Horse Artillery, 1814*

*Bombardier and Trumpeter. Horse Artillery, 1814-1816*

*Field-grade Officers. Horse Artillery, 1814-1816. (One of the field-grade officers is shown with button loops on the coat and with a Badge for Distinction on the shako.)*

1673

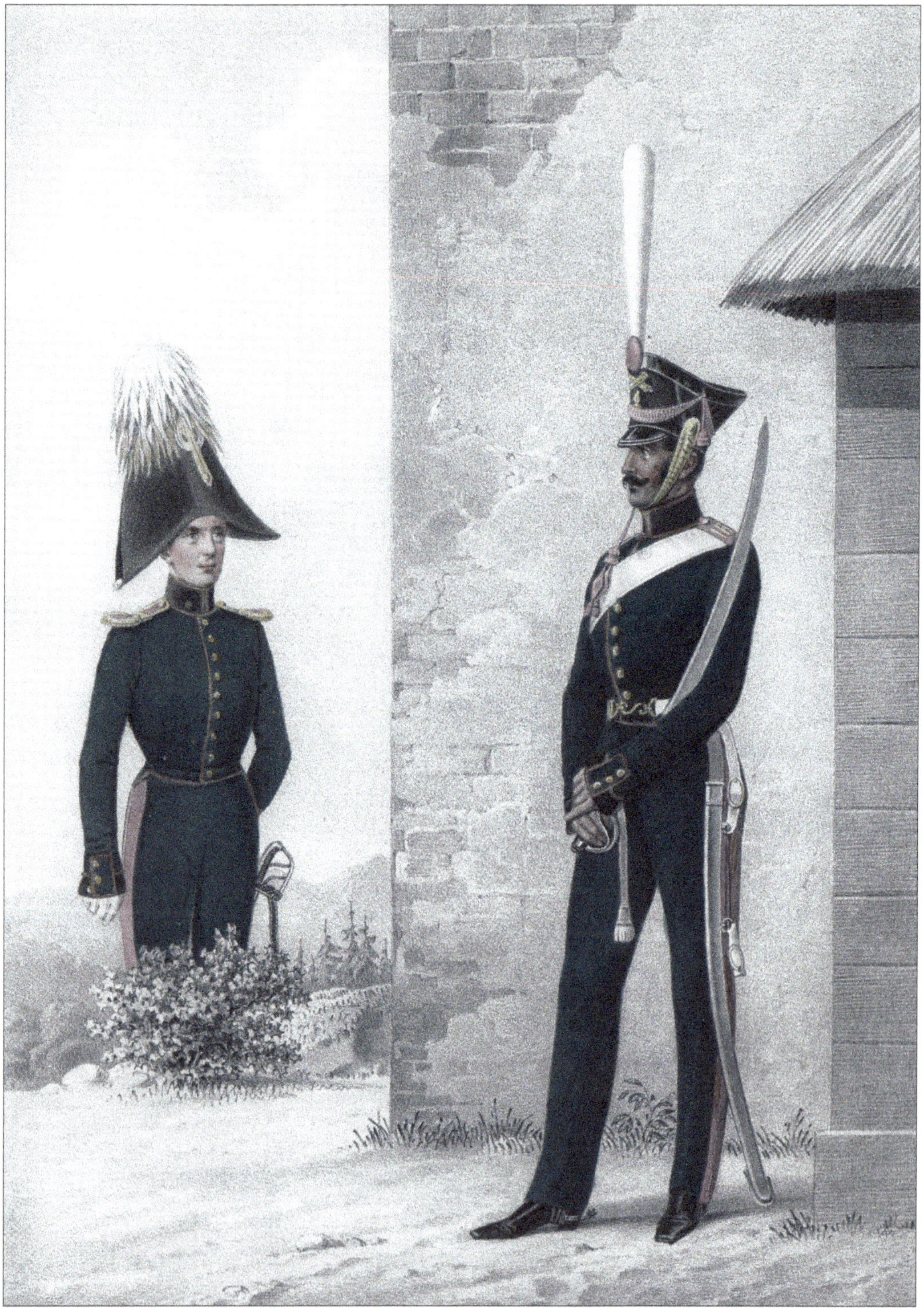

*Company-grade Officer and Cannoneer. Horse Artillery, 1816*

*Company-grade Officers. Horse Artillery, 1817-1819*

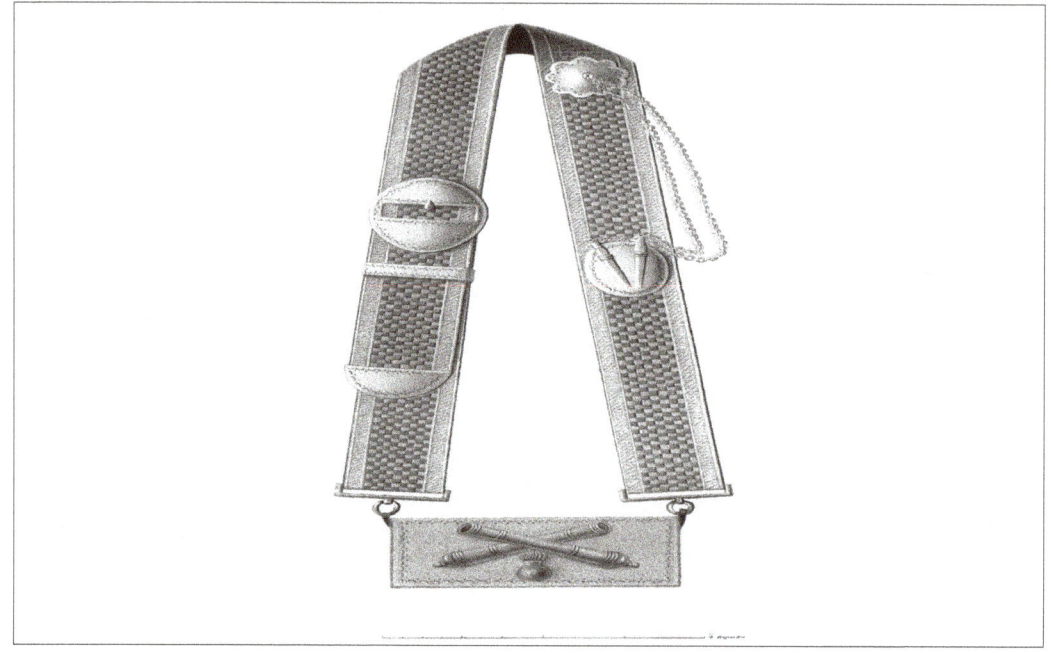

. *Pouch for Horse-Artillery Officers, established in 1817. (Note: Later, about 1821, the belt for the pouch began to be fastened no longer by rings, but in the same manner as belts for infantry pouches, as shown below in Plate No. 1708.)* -

*Forage caps for lower ranks in the Garrison Artillery, established 25 October 1811. a) Garrison companies. b) Laboratory companies. c) Fortress Commands. d) Detachments at Powder Works. e) Detachments at Permanent Arsenals. f) Detachments at Mobile Arsenals. g) Replacement Parks*

*Field-grade Officer and Bombardier. Horse Artillery of the Lithuania Corps, 1818-1825*

*Trumpeter and Company-grade Officer. Horse Artillery. 1820-1825.*

*Officer. Garrison Artillery, 1801-1802*

*Company-grade Officer, Noncommissioned Officer, and Private. Garrison Artillery, 1802-1803*

*Arsenal Warden [Tseikhvarter]. Garrison Artillery, 1802-1804*

*Noncommissioned Officer and Private. Garrison Artillery, 1803-1806*

*Master Craftsmen [Masterovye]. Powder Works, 1806-1807*

*Master Craftsmen. Powder Works, 1806-1811. (In working uniform.)*

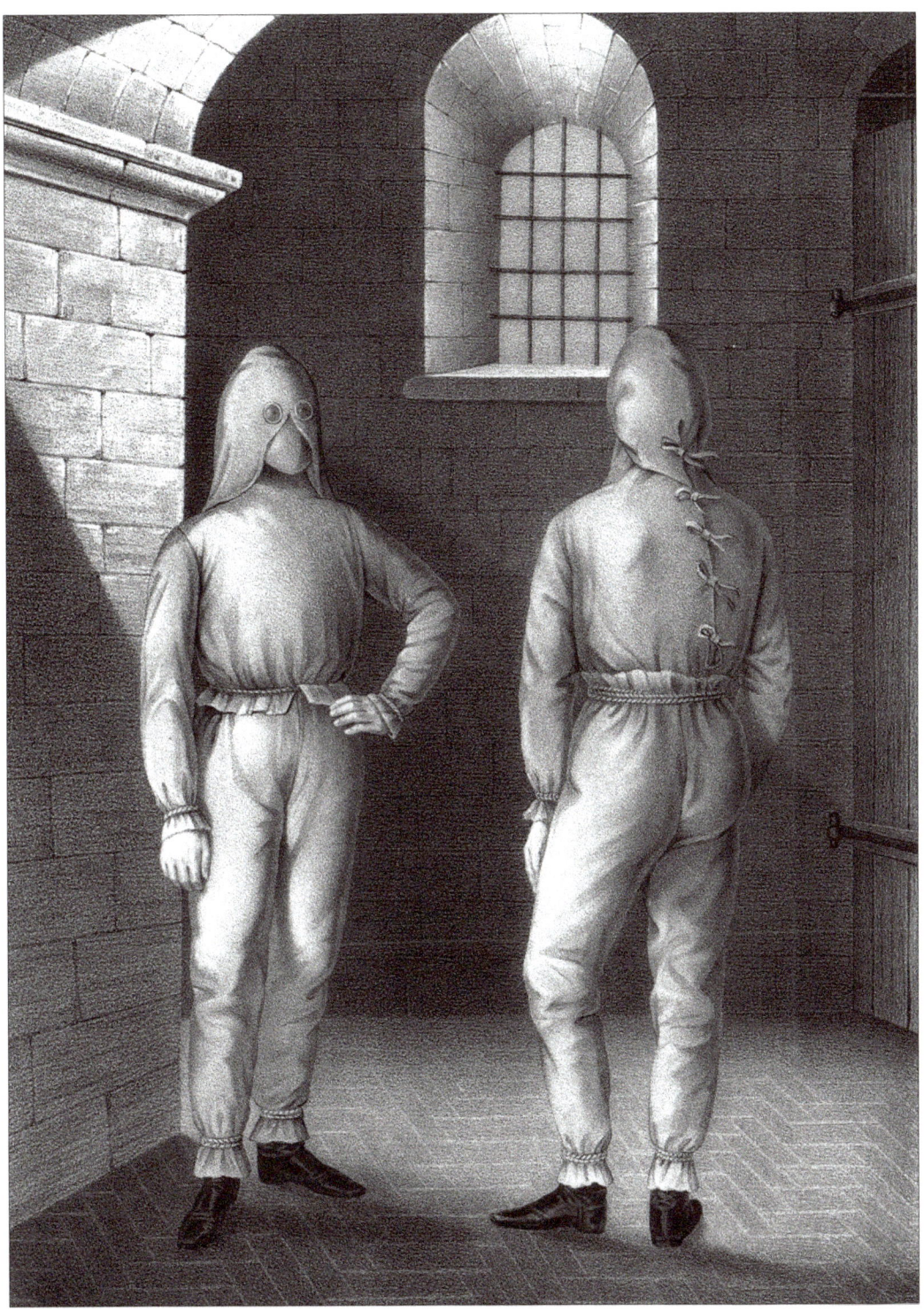

*Powder Workers [Porokhovshchiki]. Powder Works. (In working dress.)*

*Arsenal Fireworker and Private. Garrison Artillery Companies, 1808-1809*

1686

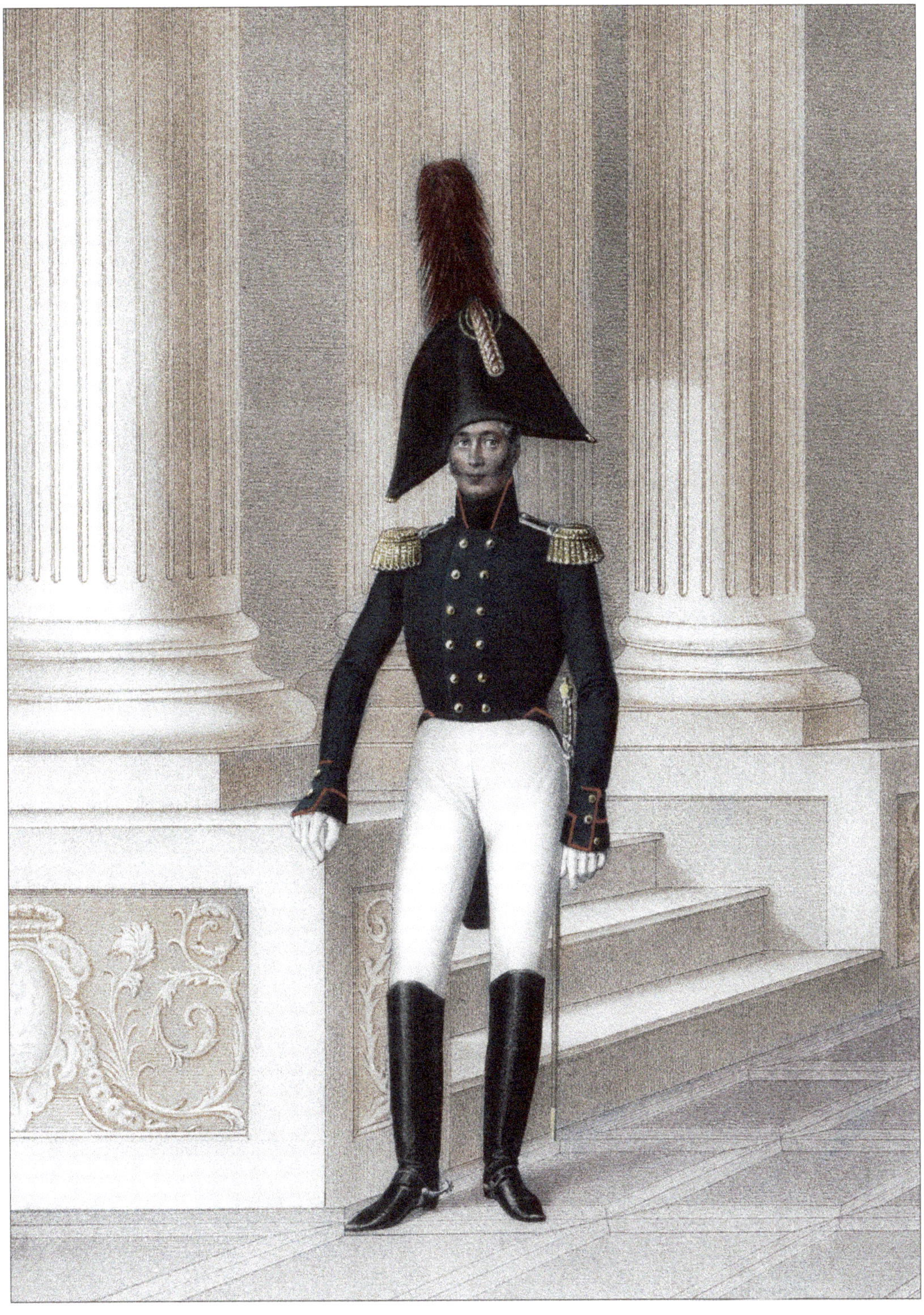

*General. Garrison Artillery, 1808-1809*

*Company-grade Officer and Private. Garrison Artillery, 1812-1816*

*Noncommissioned Officer and Company-grade Officer. Garrison Artillery, 1818-1819*

*Company-grade Officer, Cannoneer, and Drummer. Garrison Artillery, 1820-1824*

*Company-grade Officer and Noncommissioned Officer. Mobile Arsenals, 1820-1824*

*Noncommissioned Officer. Permanent Arsenals, 1820-1825*

*Private. Laboratory Companies, 1820-1825*

*Company-grade Officer. Garrison Artillery, 1822-1825*

*Private and Field-grade Officer. Garrison Artillery, 1824-1825*

*Drummer. Garrison Artillery, 1824-1825*

Сост. и рис. Пиратскій.            Лит. Главн. упрал. Путей Сообщенія и Публичн. зданій (Дир. К. Пель.)            Рис. на кам. В. Хлебаровъ.

1818 года.

Л. Гв. Измайловскій полкъ въ годъ назначенія Его Императорскаго Высочества Великаго
Князя Николая Павловича Командиромъ 2й Гвардейской Пѣхотной Бригады.

# SOLDIERS, WEAPONS & UNIFORMS ALREADY PUBLISHED
### (SEE WWW.SOLDIERSHOP.COM FOR ALL THE ISSUE)

UNIFORMS OF RUSSIAN ARMY IN THE ERA OF ANCIENT TZAR
FROM THE REIGN OF VASILI IV TO MICHAEL I, ALEXIS, FEODOR III DURING THE XVII th CENTURY
A.V.VISKOVATOV — LUCA STEFANO CRISTINI
SWU-600-004

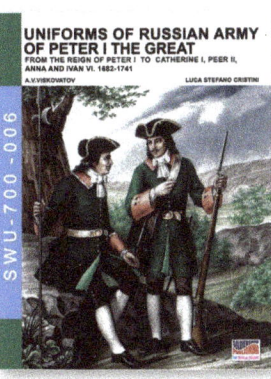

UNIFORMS OF RUSSIAN ARMY OF PETER I THE GREAT
FROM THE REIGN OF PETER I TO CATHERINE I, PEER II, ANNA AND IVAN VI. 1682-1741
A.V.VISKOVATOV — LUCA STEFANO CRISTINI
SWU-700-006

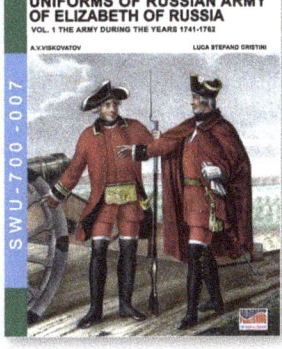

UNIFORMS OF RUSSIAN ARMY OF ELIZABETH OF RUSSIA
VOL. 1 THE ARMY DURING THE YEARS 1741-1762
A.V.VISKOVATOV — LUCA STEFANO CRISTINI
SWU-700-007

UNIFORMS OF RUSSIAN ARMY OF ELIZABETH OF RUSSIA
VOL. 2 THE ARMY DURING THE YEARS 1741-1762
A.V.VISKOVATOV — LUCA STEFANO CRISTINI
SWU-700-008

UNIFORMS OF RUSSIAN ARMY IN THE XVIII CENTURY VOL. 1
UNDER THE REIGN OF CATHERINE II EMPRESS OF RUSSIA BETWEEN 1762 AND 1796
A.V.VISKOVATOV — LUCA STEFANO CRISTINI
SWU-700-005

UNIFORMS OF RUSSIAN ARMY IN THE XVIII CENTURY VOL. 2
UNDER THE REIGN OF CATHERINE II EMPRESS OF RUSSIA BETWEEN 1762 AND 1796
A.V.VISKOVATOV — LUCA STEFANO CRISTINI
SWU-700-009

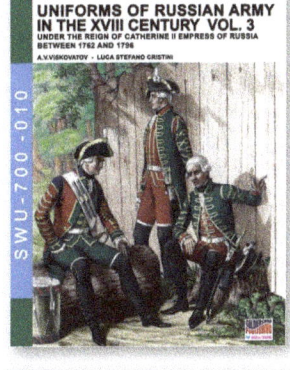

UNIFORMS OF RUSSIAN ARMY IN THE XVIII CENTURY VOL. 3
UNDER THE REIGN OF CATHERINE II EMPRESS OF RUSSIA BETWEEN 1762 AND 1796
A.V.VISKOVATOV — LUCA STEFANO CRISTINI
SWU-700-010

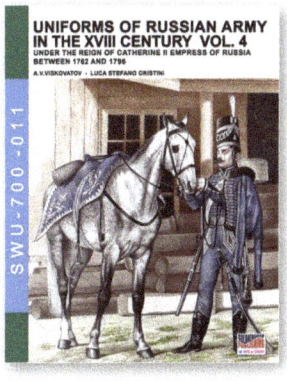

UNIFORMS OF RUSSIAN ARMY IN THE XVIII CENTURY VOL. 4
UNDER THE REIGN OF CATHERINE II EMPRESS OF RUSSIA BETWEEN 1762 AND 1796
A.V.VISKOVATOV — LUCA STEFANO CRISTINI
SWU-700-011

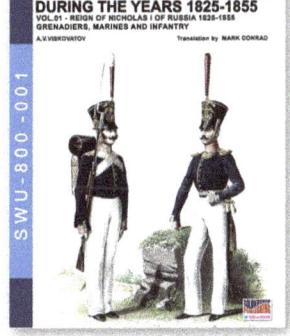

UNIFORMS OF RUSSIAN ARMY DURING THE YEARS 1825-1855
VOL.01 - REIGN OF NICHOLAS I OF RUSSIA 1825-1855 GRENADIERS, MARINES AND INFANTRY
A.V.VISKOVATOV — Translation by MARK CONRAD
SWU-800-001

UNIFORMS OF RUSSIAN ARMY DURING THE YEARS 1825-1855
VOL.02 - REIGN OF NICHOLAS I OF RUSSIA 1825-1855 CARABINIERS, JÄGERS, RIFLES, AND CUIRASSIERS
A.V.VISKOVATOV — Translation by MARK CONRAD
SWU-800-002

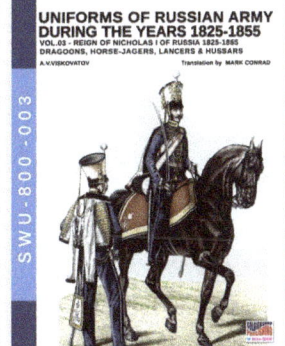

UNIFORMS OF RUSSIAN ARMY DURING THE YEARS 1825-1855
VOL.03 - REIGN OF NICHOLAS I OF RUSSIA 1825-1855 DRAGOONS, HORSE-JAGERS, LANCERS & HUSSARS
A.V.VISKOVATOV — Translation by MARK CONRAD
SWU-800-003

UNIFORMS OF RUSSIAN ARMY DURING THE YEARS 1825-1855
VOL.04 - REIGN OF NICHOLAS I OF RUSSIA 1825-1855 GENDARMES, TRAIN, ARTILLERY, SAPPERS & PIONEERS
A.V.VISKOVATOV — Translation by MARK CONRAD
SWU-800-004

UNIFORMS OF RUSSIAN ARMY DURING THE NAPOLEONIC WAR
VOL.9 - REIGN OF ALEXANDER I 1801-1825 THE INFANTRY
A.V.VISKOVATOV — TRANSLATION BY MARK CONRAD
EBOOK SWU-NAP-014

UNIFORMS OF RUSSIAN ARMY DURING THE NAPOLEONIC WAR
VOL.10 - REIGN OF ALEXANDER I OF RUSSIA 1801-1825 CAVALRY: CUIRASSIERS, DRAGOONS & HORSE-JÄGERS
A.V.VISKOVATOV — Translation by MARK CONRAD
SWU-NAP-015

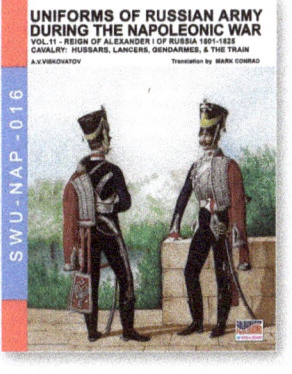

UNIFORMS OF RUSSIAN ARMY DURING THE NAPOLEONIC WAR
VOL.11 - REIGN OF ALEXANDER I OF RUSSIA 1801-1825 CAVALRY: HUSSARS, LANCERS, GENDARMES, & THE TRAIN
A.V.VISKOVATOV — Translation by MARK CONRAD
SWU-NAP-016

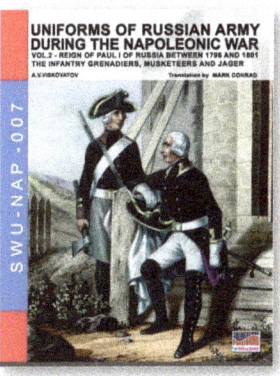

UNIFORMS OF RUSSIAN ARMY DURING THE NAPOLEONIC WAR
VOL.2 - REIGN OF PAUL I OF RUSSIA BETWEEN 1796 AND 1801 THE INFANTRY GRENADIERS, MUSKETEERS AND JAGER
A.V.VISKOVATOV — Translation by MARK CONRAD
SWU-NAP-007